Senior designer Toni Kay
Senior commissioning editor
    Annabel Morgan
Head of production
    Patricia Harrington
Art director Leslie Harrington
Editorial director Julia Charles
Publisher Cindy Richards

First published in 2020 by
Ryland Peters & Small
20–21 Jockey's Fields,
London WC1R 4BW
and
341 East 116th Street
New York, NY 10029

www.rylandpeters.com

ISBN 978-1-78879-302-5

A CIP record for this book is available from
the British Library.

Library of Congress CIP data has been
applied for.

Printed and bound in Canada

# CONTENTS

# INTRODUCTION

It was in 2010 that Prince William asked his girlfriend of eight years, Kate Middleton, to become his wife and future queen. It was also the year that Instagram was created, that Twitter allowed users to see images for the first time and Facebook reached 500 million users.

Our fascination with what the Royal Family wears is nothing new. Royals are the original celebrities. They have set trends for centuries, through all manner of upheavals, crises and wars, and their steadfast glamour has offered an anchor and been a source of joy and celebration – there is nothing, after all, quite like a royal wedding.

Fashion has forever been one of royalty's most powerful tools, a time-defying way to assert influence and communicate messages. Think of King Henry VIII's magnificently stuffed doublets, Queen Elizabeth I's extravagant ruffs or Queen Victoria's decision to wear a white wedding dress, which remains a custom to this day. And, of course, Prince William's mother Diana, Princess of Wales who dazzled the world with her fashion choices, telling the story of her extraordinary life through the medium of clothes.

When Kate Middleton stepped onto the stage, the landscape had changed beyond recognition from the genteel tradition of portraiture of centuries past. News was no longer reported day by day on the front pages of newspapers, but minute by minute via websites and social media. Anyone, anywhere in the world, could discover what Kate was wearing within an hour of her stepping out, with dozens of images capturing every outing from all imaginable angles.

In this unique combination of circumstances, the scene was set for the future Duchess of Cambridge – a sporty, middle class 'normal' girl from Berkshire – to become a new kind of royal style icon. Kate's normality was essential to conjuring her own brand of majestic magic. Her marriage to William saw her living a fairytale that many young girls had dreamed of for generations before her. This was not another aristocratic Sloane Ranger, but a girl who had been born to a flight attendant and flight dispatcher and was now destined to be Queen Consort one day.

A decade on and Kate's effect on fashion is impossible to understate – she has had dresses named after her, set trends, inspired superfans around the world and has been credited with boosting the British fashion industry by up to £1 billion in a single year.

Wasn't it inevitable that a beautiful new royal would become an influencer like no other? In a word, no. If Diana dared to experiment with fashion in a way royalty never had before, then

Kate has, over the years, created her very own royal style template, which is mindful of both the weight of history and the 21st-century prism through which her outfits are interpreted.

Kate's penchant for Zara hairbands and Topshop maternity dresses couldn't be further from the elevated costumes of royals past, but her purpose in choosing those items is exactly the same: a way to tell the world who she is and what we might like to think about her. Where Elizabeth I's armillary sphere earring in one painting signifies her divine power, so the Duchess's high street purchases portray her as relatable and democratic, allowing her fans to buy into her look – on the night she wore that Zara hairband in November 2019, it sold out within hours.

There have been glamorous evening gowns, too – many of these pieces are custom-made for the Duchess and cost thousands of pounds. These looks are not only befitting of the occasions for which they're worn, but serve as a reminder of the royals' unique place in power and politics.

The Duchess's decade as a royal has coincided with feminism dominating the zeitgeist, raising questions about what it means to be a royal woman today. When William's brother Harry married Meghan Markle in 2018, she declared herself a feminist and made working on women's issues a cornerstone of her work. Kate has not publicly declared her support for feminism, but her extensive work with children and on mental health has seen her address some of the fundamental difficulties faced by women in a more subtle way.

She has certainly been on the receiving end of commentary on the portrayal of women, which has painted her – or what she represents – in a less than flattering light. Most famous were words from a speech made by the author Hilary Mantel in 2013. She argued that Kate had been depicted as a 'jointed doll on which certain rags are hung… In those days [Kate] was a shop-window mannequin, with no personality of her own, entirely defined by what she wore.'

It's true that the Duchess's appearance is central to her appeal, a fact that might be disheartening for some. But I prefer to see fashion not as something that has obscured her real character, but a vital and potent device that she has learned to deploy with huge success. Just because it is a device used more often by women than men shouldn't detract from the influence it has nor the respect it deserves.

'Kate understood early on that fashion is a tool and that the messages it sends to draw attention to a cause are incredibly powerful, so why not capitalize on that?' says Susan Kelley, the founder of What Kate Wore, a website that has documented Kate's fashion since her marriage. 'In an ideal world, there wouldn't be fashion coverage and the discussion would be about early years or children's hospices, but the understanding was there that that's not how the world operates.'

Far from being a mere clothes horse, Kate has become fluent in the language of clothing, working out a way to look the part without allowing it to consume her. The Duchess has used it to make diplomatic gestures, to send messages of solidarity and to show respect. She has oscillated between eschewing and embracing trends. At times, her wardrobe underscores her status as wife of a future king; in the next outfit, it's all about being just like any normal British 30-something mum.

Fashion is not what defines the Duchess of Cambridge, but her clothing choices tell a captivating story about the woman who will be one of the most famous of the 21st century.

**OPPOSITE** The Duchess of Cambridge wearing a Luisa Spagnoli sweater, jeans and Superga trainers at a Heads Together reception at Kensington Palace in April 2017.

**ABOVE** The Duchess of Cambridge wearing Erdem at a dinner given by David Cains, the British Ambassador to Sweden, during the Cambridges' visit in January 2018.

OPPOSITE Kate
Middleton attends
Prince William's
passing out parade
at the Royal Military
Academy, Sandhurst
in December 2006.

# FROM KATE
## to duchess

'She was destined for that role really; she hasn't put a foot wrong,' says
Richard Ward, the hairdresser who has tended to Kate's locks since
university. 'I think she's evolved into that role seamlessly – I'm sure it
hasn't been seamless, but she makes it appear that way.'

If Kate's life story appears like a modern-day fairytale, then the time before she married William is pivotal. How do you evolve from a normal student and star hockey player to a Royal Family member so valued that you are given the Royal Victorian Order by the Queen? When your apparent fairytale contains as many twists and turns as Kate's did, from coping with life in limbo as she and William waited until their late twenties to marry to navigating a painful, albeit brief, break-up in the glare of the public eye, the evolution becomes even more compelling.

Anyone who has spent time with Kate always returns to one fundamental aspect of her personality: her resolute, quietly confident sense of self. 'She's got a sense of her own style. It doesn't feel like she's been swayed by anyone or anything, she's just her own person,' adds Ward. 'I think that's what's won her through.'

Daniella Helayel of Issa, Kate's go-to designer during her twenties and the creator of her famous engagement dress, recalls her being 'a wonderful girl. She's as good as you can get.' This sweetness and light, coupled with a generous soupçon of determination, is the strategy that saw Kate through the girlfriend years, as evidenced by the looks that exhibit her steady transformation into a future queen on her own terms.

# THE DRESS THAT LAUNCHED A ROYAL ROMANCE, MARCH 2002

Legend has it that the sparks of William and Kate's romance were ignited on 26 March 2002, when the Prince bought a front-row seat at the St Andrews University Charity Fashion Show. At this point they were friends, but it was a gossamer-fine, slip-of-a-thing dress, designed by textiles student Charlotte Todd, that would set Kate on the path to joining the Royal Family. When Kate sashayed out in the gold and black silk see-through design, William reportedly turned to his friend Fergus Boyd and said, 'Wow, Fergus, Kate's hot!'

'I think the dress showed the "naughty" side of the Duchess,' says auctioneer Kerry Taylor, who would go on to sell the dress nine years later. 'Charlotte intended the transparent garment to be worn as a skirt with a slip underneath. The fact that Kate chose to wear it as a dress perhaps indicates not only her intention to grab the Prince's attention, which it obviously did, but her sense of fun. Charlotte had no idea that her student piece would create such a stir. Kate's athletic figure certainly looked great in it.'

Images of Kate in the LBD shot to fame once the royal romance was revealed, depicting her as an adventurous risk-taker and allowing the world to see her in the same way William had that night – though the story is undoubtedly more nuanced than one sudden moment of attraction.

Todd had made the skirt/dress for a project entitled The Art of Seduction as part of her course at the University of the West of England, and sent it in response to a request for pieces for the St Andrews show, unaware that her creation would go on to play a role in history. Weeks before Kate and William's eventual marriage, Todd decided to part with her design, entrusting its sale to Taylor.

'I will never forget that auction – the room was packed to bursting,' Taylor remembers. 'We had telephone and commission bids, but suddenly a young man put up his hand and started bidding. He was taking bidding instructions on his mobile phone and there was a murmur of excitement in the room as the price crept upwards. Who was on the other end of that mobile was anyone's guess. Many of the press assumed it was Prince William. When I banged down the hammer in favour of the unknown bidder, he started to be mobbed by the press pack. I jumped off the rostrum and got my staff to take him to safety in the back office. Once the sale was over, I sneaked him out of a back door, but a TV cameraman spotted us and soon the whole press mob was in hot pursuit but we managed to get him away. It wasn't purchased by Prince William but by a collector of celebrity memorabilia who purchased it as an investment.'

All that is known about the purchaser is that he was identified as 'Nick from Jersey'. He paid $65,000 for the barely-there dress. Taylor remembers him saying, 'Just think – one day I can say this was worn by the Queen of England!'

As for Kate, she has only once commented publicly on the dress that allegedly determined the course of her life. 'I hope you weren't involved in the fashion show,' she said to a group of St Andrews students in 2012 at the university's 600th anniversary charity celebration. 'You never know what you are going to be asked to wear.'

# THE ROYAL GIRLFRIEND, DECEMBER 2006

The early years of Kate and William's relationship were mostly shrouded in secrecy. But when the Prince passed out from Sandhurst, having completed his Army officer training, the opportunity was taken to confirm that Middleton was special. It's hardly surprising that engagement rumours began to swirl after her appearance at the parade, where she appeared a consummate princess-in-training.

It was a bitterly cold winter day but Kate showed grit by not bundling up in unphotogenic layers. Instead she chose a bold scarlet coat that coordinated with the red details on William's Number 1 ceremonial uniform. Aged 25 at the time, she looked poised if a little beyond her years in the Armani design (see page 10).

Wearing a wide-brimmed black hat created by leading milliner Philip Treacy proved that Kate was already well versed in the royal requirement to rise to the occasion. Indeed, she has gone on to re-wear it twice as a Duchess, in 2012 and 2017. She also re-wore the coat in 2013.

If Kate's outfit suggested that she was preparing to assume an official royal role, there was still evidence that this was also a simple case of girl loves boy. 'I love the uniform,' Kate was overheard saying to her mother as they watched the parade, 'It's so, so sexy.'

**LEFT** Kate on the catwalk in a Charlotte Todd dress at the St Andrews University Charity Fashion Show, 2002.

# THE BREAK-UP DRESS, MAY 2007

Hopes of an imminent royal wedding were dashed when news broke that William and Kate had ended their relationship in April 2007 and Kate faced the prospect of negotiating life as a young single woman who had not long ago seemed on the verge of becoming royal. Just a couple of months later, she transformed her image, showing William what he was missing.

Kate's most powerful display of what might be called revenge dressing came at a book launch in May. With Pippa in tow, Kate opted for a lace shift dress by Australian designer Collette Dinnigan. Complemented by her relaxed blow-dry, there was a lingerie feel to the outfit that was at once elegant and just daring enough. Within months, Kate and William had rekindled their romance, and though a wedding was still a way off, there was now clarity and security.

# THE ROLLER DISCO, SEPTEMBER 2008

If commentators had assumed that, with a future as a royal wife practically assured, Kate Middleton would appear demure and appropriate at all times, she confounded them by embracing the day-glo dress code for a fundraising roller disco in 2008.

There are countless shots from this time of Kate in sweet summer dresses and skirt suits, so Middleton in party girl mode, enjoying a night with friends rather than being concerned with protocols, was an exciting departure.

Several aspects of the evening grabbed headlines, from Kate's yellow hotpants to her sequined halter-neck top to her dramatic flop onto the dance floor. There was one concession to discretion, however: she sported glossy nude tights with her shorts and fuchsia legwarmers.

The appeal of seeing Kate like this is simple. It reveals a natural, joyful side of her personality, unaffected by duty or formalities – especially meaningful now that she is a decade into royal life and one of the most popular senior members of the Royal Family.

## THE WEDDING GUEST LOOK, OCTOBER 2010

A quintessential Kate Middleton genre of dressing was the wedding-guest look. In the pre-engagement years, the nuptials of friends and relatives were prime opportunities to spot William's girlfriend. Kate's outfits reflected her natural elegance and a consciousness that, while photographers might have turned out for a glimpse of her, she was determined not to upstage the bride.

One of these outings was the wedding of their friend Harry Meade to Rosemarie Bradford at St Peter and St Paul's church in Gloucestershire. Kate and William arrived together, tanned after a holiday in Kenya.

Having been introduced to designer Daniella Helayel by a friend in 2005, her label Issa had become a favourite of Kate's. Now she turned to Issa for a knee-length cobalt dress teamed with a black nipped-waist jacket and suede heels. Charmingly, Kate's saucer hat had been rented for $100 from loan service Get Ahead Hats.

Less than a month later, the reason for Kate and William's

evident happiness would be revealed. And an even more iconic Issa dress would be born.

**OPPOSITE ABOVE**  Kate and Pippa at the book launch for Simon Sebag Montefiore's *Young Stalin*, May 2007.

**OPPOSITE BELOW** Kate on skates at the Day-Glo Midnight Roller Disco fundraiser, September 2008.

**ABOVE** Kate and Prince William at the wedding of Harry Meade and Rosemarie Bradford, October 2010.

for the official photocall in a £385 silk jersey wrap dress by Issa. Its inky blue shade coordinated meticulously with the ring: 14 solitaire diamonds surrounding a 12-carat oval blue Ceylon sapphire that had been created by Garrard in 1981 as engagement ring for William's mother Diana, and was inspired by the 'something blue' brooch given to Queen Victoria by Prince Albert to celebrate their wedding in 1840.

The response was immediate and dramatic for Issa – the design sold out, press interest in the label skyrocketed and high-street brands rushed to create affordable imitations. 'That dress had been in my collection since 2005,' Daniella Helayel says, 'but now it was on the cover of every newspaper and magazine. Sales went through the roof.'

Would any dress have had the same effect? No. There was something about the Issa. It made Kate look glamorous yet respectful; she wasn't trying to seem more mature than she was, but nor did the dress depict her as a slave to fashion.

Although Issa later ran into trouble, Helayel hopes that the women who loved her designs still treasure and wear them now. 'I didn't want to do fashion,' she reflects. 'I wanted to do clothing that people could leave for their daughters.' Perhaps one day we'll see the royal Issa once again on Princess Charlotte?

# THE ENGAGEMENT DRESS

On 16 November 2010, St James's Palace confirmed the engagement of Prince William and Miss Catherine Middleton. It was the culmination of a long relationship, drawn out to allow the couple years of relative freedom and privacy before taking on the pressures of royal duties.

Kate's style had already captivated the public, but that interest went stratospheric when she stepped out

# THE DUCHESS-IN-TRAINING LOOK

Between the engagement and the wedding, Kate and William toured the UK carrying out a select few visits to gently introduce the Duchess-to-be to royal duties. For most of these appearances, Kate opted for unfussy looks mostly sourced from her existing wardrobe.

If this strategy felt a little lacklustre after all the excitement of the engagement, then reassurance arrived in early March when the couple spent the day in Belfast. Here, Kate eschewed her comfort zone in favour of a fluted hem trench coat by Burberry. As the world-famous inventor of the trench, the choice was a brilliant example of her opportunity to dust off British powerhouse names and show them off afresh to the world with new royal gleam.

**ABOVE** Prince William and Kate Middleton visit Belfast City Hall in March 2011. Kate wears a trench from Burberry.

**RIGHT** Kate, her mother and sister arrive at The Goring hotel, London, on 28 April 2011, the day before her wedding to Prince William.

# THE WEDDING EVE LOOK

Kate's final look as a single woman and commoner was the epitome of everything the world had come to know of her. In true Kate fashion, she didn't invest in a new outfit for the final wedding rehearsal and her arrival at The Goring hotel – where she was to spend the night before the wedding – instead choosing an Issa dress that she'd owned since 2006 and a ruffle cream jacket by BCBG Max Azria. A classic Kate finishing touch came courtesy of her patent espadrille wedges by L.K. Bennett.

The following day, she would be a royal bride, complete with gown and tiara, but in this moment, she was the girl next door whose story had gripped people across the globe.

# THE WEDDING DAY
## *The Dress*

Kate's choice of wedding dress brilliantly encapsulates the delicate balance she has struck throughout her royal life between catering to her personal tastes while acknowledging the unique significance of her position. On her wedding day, the personal and the patriotic were in impressive equilibrium.

In the months leading up to the marriage, the rumour mill was in overdrive regarding the identity of the Duchess-to-be's chosen wedding dress designer. And mostly the press underestimated her, taking her conservative, ladylike style as a cue that she would commission a 'safe' name or an established specialist in classic bridal gowns – Jenny Packham, Phillipa Lepley and Bruce Oldfield were all contenders, as was Sophie Cranston, designer of small label Libélula, which had become a recent favourite of Kate's at the time.

But this school of thought had completely forgotten that Kate was a graduate in Art History, with a far more nuanced appreciation for the importance of craft and design than many might have given her credit for. Indeed, *Vogue*'s then editor Alexandra Shulman was summoned to Clarence House to offer her professional opinion.

'We sat on a sofa and discussed the various options, piles of pictures scattered on the floor,' Shulman recalled in her book *Clothes.... And Other Things That Matter*. 'As we talked, I began to realize that my favourite was Alexander

**ABOVE RIGHT** The wedding day – 28 April 2011. Kate arriving at Westminster Abbey accompanied by her maid of honour, sister Pippa Middleton.

McQueen, a label which at that point, shortly after McQueen's horribly untimely death, was newly in the hands of Sarah Burton. I thought that the level of extraordinary craftsmanship and their tradition of working with symbolism would be up to the task, that Sarah and Catherine would get on as women and that it would be terrific to have a relatively untraditional fashion

house given this privilege. And then I left. I didn't mention the meeting to anyone and I didn't hear anything more.'

The Alexander McQueen name might also have been in Kate's orbit after seeing the subtly unconventional McQueen creation that Sara Buys, a fashion writer, wore to marry Tom Parker Bowles (son of Camilla) in 2005. Although Sara

denied ever having given Kate advice, that design's striking point of difference may have offered some inspiration.

'You want to do a dream dress,' considers Elizabeth Emanuel, who along with her then husband David created Princess Diana's legendary wedding gown. 'But then you have to consider that, as it's a royal bride, it's going to be part of history. In every royal wedding dress, there's a message in there as well.'

When Kate stepped out of the Rolls Royce Phantom VI at Westminster Abbey just before 11am on 29 April 2011, she created one of the great fashion moments of the 21st century. The McQueen name had been rumoured in the run-up to the wedding, but confirmation that the future Queen had chosen the house sent the fashion industry into raptures.

'Miss Middleton chose British brand Alexander McQueen for the beauty of its craftsmanship and its respect for traditional workmanship and the technical construction of clothing,' read the official press release about the gown. 'Miss Middleton wished for her dress to combine tradition and modernity with the artistic vision that characterizes Alexander McQueen's work.'

Like the Queen, Kate ensured that British symbols were incorporated into the design, with rose, thistle, daffodil and shamrock motifs appearing on the gown's lace elements. Comparisons were also made with the dress that Grace Kelly wore to marry Prince Rainier of Monaco in 1956, thanks especially to the slim lace sleeves and elevated neckline, which offered a sense of classical grandeur. The gown's most distinctively McQueen flourish was its understated but unusual Victorian-style bustle.

'The dress showed that Kate was not painting herself as a fashion icon,' observes Emanuel. 'It's very traditional and wasn't going out on a limb. Something very high fashion would have been wrong – Sarah got it absolutely right, it was beautiful. Everyone was so excited to see the dress, but what was lovely was that it showed off Kate.'

Kate's choice may not have been a design that rewrote the wedding dress rulebook, but it marked an assured transition from commoner to royal and delivered a firm message that the new Duchess was ready to explore the possibilities of fashion. Copies of Burton's creation were made within hours and it evoked a renaissance of demure, timeless bridal gowns. What's more, it marked the beginning not only of a royal marriage but a fashion partnership between Kate and McQueen that endures a decade on.

## Wedding dress facts

The lace appliqué was handmade by the Royal School of Needlework, based at Hampton Court Palace.

The Carrickmacross lace-making technique, which originated in Ireland in the 1820s, was used.

Seamstresses washed their hands every 30 minutes to keep the lace and threads pristine. Needles were replaced every three hours to keep them sharp and clean.

Something blue: Burton's team sewed a blue ribbon into the lining of the dress.

Train length: 270 cm/106 in compared to Diana's 762 cm/300 in.

OPPOSITE The newly married couple emerge from Westminster Abbey followed by a cluster of bridesmaids in simple off-white ballerina-length dresses with pale gold sashes by childrenswear designer Nicki Macfarlane.

**ABOVE** Kate wore the Queen's Cartier Halo tiara on her wedding day with an ivory silk tulle veil and new diamond earrings by Robinson Pelham, a gift from her parents.

## THE JEWELLERY

No royal wedding is complete without a tiara. In keeping with the restrained elegance of her wedding dress, Kate chose to borrow the Halo tiara, created in 1936 by Cartier and comprising 16 graduated scrolls, set with 739 brilliants and 149 baton diamonds. It was purchased by the Queen's father, the then Duke of York, to give to her mother just weeks before the abdication crisis brought them to the throne, and later the Queen was given the tiara as an 18th birthday gift.

The Middleton family was represented via a pair of diamond earrings by Robinson Pelham featuring diamond-set oak leaves with a pear-shaped diamond drop and a pavé-set diamond acorn suspended in the centre. The design was inspired by the acorns and oak leaves in the Middleton coat of arms, which was created in the run-up to the wedding. The earrings, a gift from Kate's parents, were made to work alongside the tiara.

## THE HAIRDRESSER'S VIEW – *Richard Ward*

'We had been doing Kate's hair as far back as her university days, so we already knew her well. She was obviously a long-haired girl and I think she wanted to have a resemblance of how she normally looked, so that's why we opted for a half-up, half-down style – the best of both worlds. Once we realized that she was going to be wearing a tiara, and a pretty heavy one, it was much safer to have some of the hair up, to wrap around it and secure it – like a safety net. Knowing that billions of people around the world would be looking at her, we wanted to keep the hair off the face.

The day itself was surreal. We looked after all of the bridal party – we had 10 of our team at The Goring that day. It was a privilege to be in the room with Kate in the morning, especially with banks of press and crowds outside.

Although we had practised it a thousand times, the pressure was huge. The feeling of elation when Kate came out just after they were married and we realized that everything had stayed in place, nothing had fallen down and the bridesmaids' hair was as it was meant to be – that was an incredible feeling, when you know you've nailed it.'

## THE EVENING LOOK

'She wanted to be natural,' says Richard Ward of Kate's simple directive for the evening reception. After a day of pomp and circumstance celebrating the marriage of a future king, the evening celebration was about Kate and William themselves, marking their marriage with 300 close friends and family.

Many said that the look Kate picked for the evening was what she might have chosen for the main ceremony had she not been marrying into the Royal Family. But there was a simple glamour to the dress, also created by Sarah Burton at Alexander McQueen. With its crystal belt, the design was distinctly 'evening', while the full skirt and fitted bodice reflected the silhouette of the day gown.

The most endearing part of the images that were released on the night was the Duchess's fluffy mohair bolero cardigan, a sweet concession to practicality and a nod to her usual safe personal style. But perhaps, too, a way to keep a little of the look private – the outfit may have read quite differently once she arrived at Buckingham Palace and peeled off that layer as she partied into the night with her new husband, surrounded by the friends and family who had helped carry them to that day.

**LEFT** The Duchess of Cambridge leaves Clarence House in her Alexander McQueen gown to travel to Buckingham Palace for the evening reception.

**OPPOSITE** Kate chose Reiss's Shola dress to meet Michelle Obama at Buckingham Palace, May 2011.

# the KATE EFFECT

It has long been an unspoken expectation that the Royal Family will fly the flag for British fashion. The women who came before Kate did this by commissioning the country's best designers and dressmakers to create their wardrobes, a tradition that she's continued.

The Duchess's decision to also wear affordable, ready-to-wear pieces that are available to buy has only amplified that impact to astonishing levels; estimates of the value that Kate adds to the industry vary wildly, with figures between £152 million and £1 billion being mooted. Ask any designer or label she's worn and they all agree that Kate has a magic touch. It's a phenomenon that's come to be known as the Kate Effect.

'She's really loved in the US, so that's where a lot of orders came from,' says Indian designer Anita Dongre, whose business enjoyed unprecedented attention when Kate wore one of her dresses in Mumbai in 2016. Her website crashed and stock quickly sold out, but Dongre created a waiting list to get the £150 dress to as many fans as possible.

Labels big and small, across all price points, report the same eruption of interest when the Duchess is pictured wearing one of their designs; British occasionwear specialist Needle & Thread said it had an 800-strong waiting list for its £410 Aurora dress after the Duchess first wore the label publicly in 2020, while Irish outdoor brand Dubarry reported a spike in website traffic, sales and footfall in its stores when Kate wore its £399 tweed Bracken jacket in 2019.

'The first time the Duchess wore Eponine was a day we will never forget,' says Jet Shenkman, the founder of one of Kate's more under-the-radar discoveries, Eponine London, which specializes in 'tailored chic and timeless pieces'. The Duchess debuted a red checked two-piece by the label to visit a mentoring programme in 2016.

'The phone started ringing within minutes and orders came through that we could have never dreamed of,' Shenkman confides. 'In those days we were still working from a tiny studio in the basement of my home, with just one tailor, and we were totally unprepared for the response. It was fabulous and we will forever be grateful to the Duchess. The press we received put our tiny business on a broader map.'

One of the first brands to benefit from the influence of the Kate Effect was Reiss. The Duchess-to-be emphasized her desire to support the high street when she chose the label's £159 Nanette dress, along with a Whistles blouse, to wear in her engagement portraits. 'Kate has been a Reiss customer for many years now and for her to choose to wear one of our dresses for such a wonderful occasion, announcing her engagement, we were over the moon,' the brand's founder, David Reiss, remembers.

Kate's breath-of-fresh-air approach to royal dressing was confirmed via two more big Reiss moments. On her first royal tour to Canada in June 2011, she re-wore the Nanette dress for a military ceremony – the sort of setting where a bespoke look might once have been expected. This came a few weeks after Kate and William had made their first appearance after their honeymoon, meeting Barack and Michelle Obama at Buckingham Palace, for which the new Duchess chose Reiss's cappuccino-hued Shola dress – an apt choice to be pictured with the First Lady, who had made J.Crew a White House norm.

At these moments, the Kate Effect was unprecedented. 'From a sales perspective, specifically looking back at the moments Kate wore the Nanette dress and the Shola dress, we were inundated with enquiries,' notes Reiss.

'With the Shola dress, the surge in web traffic caused our website to crash. And once we were back up and running, at one point we were selling one per minute until it had completely sold out. In the US it sold out before stores even opened their doors, with people calling our customer services number and buying over the phone.'

This Kate fashion frenzy helped to put Reiss on the fashion map. 'There is no question that Kate choosing to wear Reiss over the years has positively impacted the brand,' says Reiss, who saw profits double at his company in the year following Kate's early outings in the label.

It wasn't just Reiss that Kate helped to conquer America. Another of her go-to labels (most famously for nude high heels) became L.K. Bennett, which was able to open in New York in 2012 thanks in part to Kate's help in raising the brand's profile. 'Kate Middleton is an elegant lady, she wears our clothing and our shoes very well and the American public are infatuated with her, which has definitely helped us, being new to the American market,' L.K. Bennett's US president Tony DiMasso, told *The Guardian*.

In the decade that saw the rise of the fashion influencer as a career for so many, the Duchess of Cambridge has arguably out-influenced them all, creating a look that's become a cultural touchpoint and source of inspiration for millions of women.

**OPPOSITE** The Duke and Duchess of Cambridge visit Ottawa, Canada, July 2011. Kate is wearing the Reiss Nanette dress she chose for her engagement portraits.

**PAGE 29** Kate in Eponine London for a visit to the youth charity XLP in London, March 2016.

# Meet the RepliKates

The Duchess of Cambridge's style has become a topic of fascination for many, but none more so than her faithful 'repliKates'. These women embody the Kate Effect in its purest form, seeking to emulate the Duchess's style head to toe. When they cannot source the exact pieces that Kate has worn, they scour the shops for close matches. Like Kate herself, the 'repliKates' have become social media sensations, attracting thousands of followers in their journey to dress like a duchess.

## Janelle Nash from Scotsdale, Arizona @royalreplikate

I first became interested in the Duchess of Cambridge's style in 2009 when Prince William and Kate, as she was then known then, were dating. I love that Catherine wears classic fashion that is timeless, elegant and ladylike.

I started sharing my 'repliKate' looks on Instagram way back in 2010, and my reason for doing so was to connect with other 'repliKaters' in the spirit of mutual admiration and sharing our finds. Many years later my focus has changed slightly; the astronomical growth in the repliKate community and the changes that come with that growth mean it has evolved and the community is markedly different now. Social media expansion and the 24/7 news cycle mean that there is a frenzied rush to purchase a fashion item the second it is identified before it sells out, which leads to much competition. But times change and those who are dedicated long-time royal fashion watchers adapt.

**First repliKate item:** The pretty cornflower blue Zara pleated dress that she wore for her going away on her honeymoon photos. I still love and wear this dress.

**Favourite repliKate item:** My Temperley Odele coat. I wanted the coat as soon as Kate had worn it, but the big-ticket price was disconcerting. Then my husband surprised me with a trip to London and I was able to find the coat at a very steep discount!

**Favourite Kate looks:** My first choice is her royal wedding fashion, both her wedding and what she wore to Pippa's wedding. My second choice is what she wears on royal tours.

## Mallory Johnson from Washington DC @lady.m.replikates

I began informally 'repliKating' around 2011, around the time of the royal wedding. Even though Kate is one of the most famous figures in the world, many of her fashion choices are those of a normal person. It's refreshingly down to earth when Kate wears something that is obtainable, such as Zara, Topshop, Hobbs or L.K. Bennett. When she wears something that is more 'high street', there is the opportunity to own a piece of sartorial history.

More than anything, the style of the Duchess of Cambridge was a legitimization of my personal style. It was a way that I could channel the clothes I felt comfortable in, with Kate serving as an inspiration. I think Kate has made timeless, elegant fashion relatable and I am immensely appreciative to have a style icon with such grace and class.

I stumbled upon the 'repliKate' community in 2017 when I found a few Instagram accounts of other ladies sharing their royal wardrobes, so I thought it might be fun if I did, too. Over several years, the community has expanded to include some of the loveliest people. As a group, many of us took a course through the University of Glasgow and Historic Royal Palaces on the History of Royal Fashion, which was fascinating and provided a level of substance to royal style watching.

**First repliKate item:** The Zara chiffon dress Kate wore leaving Buckingham Palace on her way to her honeymoon the day after the wedding.

**Proudest finds:** I have had some excellent luck with some of the handbags Kate has worn. I have found her Smythson Panama East West tote, her Mulberry Polly Push Lock bag and her Tod's D-Bag.

**Favourite Kate looks:** I love both ends of the spectrum – the gowns and tiaras for glamorous formal occasions like state dinners, but then also her casual, country-chic looks that are so relatable.

**Still searching for:** Kate's Paul & Joe Lyrisme cape from the royal tour to Bhutan.

## Susan Kelley from Michigan
*www.whatkatewore.com*

My husband and I ran a retail store called Preppy Princess, and any time we had anything related to Kate, it was super-popular. That's how the idea for a blog began. I started posting in March 2011, but it really started to take off during Kate and William's tour to Canada and America after the wedding because that put her on the world stage.

The one word I think of when I think of Kate is 'appropriate'. She clearly has tremendous respect for the monarchy as an institution and family, and she's not going to do anything inappropriate. She's so thoughtful about what she represents. A lot of people have a vision about how fun and enjoyable it must be to be trying on clothes and putting on outfits, but I'm pretty sure the reality is that it's not.

Back when I started, I could spend a few hours hunting for something and I'd feel so elated when I finally found that Joseph tweed jacket. Now 90% of the time these genius women on Twitter and Instagram identify things in seconds. It's crazy.

It can be gruelling to run the blog, especially when they go on tour somewhere like Australia and New Zealand. You have to flip your schedule – and drink a lot of Diet Coke. The hours can be brutal, but how lucky am I to be doing this?

**OPPOSITE** Kate in a Zara double-breasted blazer at a wine tasting in Otago, New Zealand, April 2014.

# DUCHESS of
# the high street

When Anna Harvey, *Vogue* fashion editor and stylist to Diana, Princess of Wales, was asked whether she had considered introducing high-street clothing to the royal wardrobe, her response was a categorical no. Diana's sartorial focus was nearly always on designer and bespoke.

Diana had blasted away many regal dressing conventions, but the idea that royal women's public wardrobes might be easy for the rest of us to emulate or that they should contain pieces costing tens, rather than thousands, of pounds was not one of them.

By the time that Kate Middleton arrived on the scene, the landscape had shifted. There was now a plethora of great quality, stylish labels on the British high street, and the dawn of online shopping, news websites and social media meant that any item could be found and bought at the click of a mouse. If a picture of Kate dashing around Chelsea in a French Connection dress was taken in the morning, women the world over could 'get the look' later that day.

Unlike Diana, who had a typically meagre teenage pre-marriage wardrobe, Kate had enjoyed years of creating her own style and shopping; she worked as an assistant buyer at Jigsaw, one of the UK's more upscale high-street retailers, and was often spotted browsing on the King's Road, Chelsea, picking up affordable buys that she was later pictured wearing to work or parties. When Kate and William became engaged, her penchant for wearing high street was integral to her appeal; she was a 'normal' girl and we knew that because she wore 'normal' clothes.

In tandem with Kate's well-developed high-street nous, sentiments about the Royal Family had altered. There was less public appetite for princesses with wardrobes crammed with couture. Affection for the Windsors was still high, especially once Kate and William's love story was made official, but a scandal could erupt at any suggestion of overspending or ostentation.

Although the Queen had always justified clothing expenditure as part of her work uniform or costume, and there were few official prices to put on her wardrobe, as most of it is created in-house by her team of dressers, it was quickly evident that it would be a master-stroke in public relations for this new-generation duchess to charm with thrifty fashion choices.

When Marie-Antoinette abandoned her sumptuous silks in favour of a simple, gauzy cotton gown inspired by rural farming attire in a 1783 portrait by Élisabeth Louise Vigée Le Brun, she had provoked uproar in France. Almost 250 years on in Britain, another royal tastemaker's decision to wear items that were accessible to her subjects had the opposite effect – it was endearing and cleverly cost-conscious. Let them shop in Zara!

From her royal girlfriend years to now, Kate has continued her long-held affection for scouting out a bargain, rewriting centuries of protocol and modernising the public's relationship with the Royal Family.

Her high-street purchases have carried her through all kinds of engagements; she's worn Boden to visit a children's hospital, Marks & Spencer to pay tribute to the emergency services, L.K. Bennett to host a US President and Whistles for a portrait unveiling. Kate also has a knack for high/low dressing, pairing a Banana Republic skirt and Goat blouse, an Alexander McQueen coat with a Zara dress and a Warehouse sweater with a Chanel handbag.

For some of her earlier looks, the Duchess even went beyond the high street in her search for low-cost pieces. For outings with the Queen in March and June 2012, she wore a blue tweed coat from M by Missoni found at Bicester Village, the designer discount outlet in Oxfordshire. By wearing such a frugal purchase twice in the company of Her Majesty, the Duchess managed to be at once understated and the fashion story of the day. Later that year, Kate confirmed her love for Bicester to the wife of a Singaporean government minister. She's been spotted browsing there several times, buying everything from baby clothes to handbags.

Another display of thrift came when Kate wore a dress by defunct label Jesiré to the National Portrait Gallery in

**ABOVE** Kate in a red Boden coat on a visit to London's Great Ormond Street Hospital in January 2018.

**OPPOSITE** For a 2012 outing with the Queen and Camilla, Kate chose a blue coat by M by Missoni from designer outlet Bicester Village.

February 2012, immediately sparking a hunt to discover its provenance. It later emerged that she had sent an assistant to browse at The Stock Exchange, a second-hand store near her family home in Berkshire, a move that was thrilling in its normality, but frustrating for the Kate fans who wanted to copy the look.

There's evidence that the Duchess and her stylists are avid online shoppers, too. In December 2016, she wore a £170 cashmere sweater from Iris & Ink, the in-house label of discount site The Outnet, for a Scouts Christmas party. It was a relatable style gesture at a time of year when many women resort to shopping online as a quick fix.

In recent years, Kate has used more affordable pieces to experiment and introduce new silhouettes. She's also added new labels into the mix, including French-girl favourites Sandro and Sézane, which have lent a more exciting edge to her royal uniform. Her message? You don't need to spend a fortune to look good.

**LEFT** Wearing top-to-toe high street at the King's Cup Regatta on the Isle of Wight in August 2019.

# Kate's favourite high-street store: Zara

Like millions of 30-somethings the world over, Kate's Zara habit has not waned over the years and it's become her most-worn high-street label.

One of Kate's most powerful statements of the kind of royal she would be came on the day after her wedding. Following the grandeur of her Alexander McQueen wedding gown and Cartier Halo tiara, she strolled through the grounds of Buckingham Palace hand in hand with Prince William wearing a floaty blue dress by Zara. She may no longer have been a commoner, but the look displayed a clever common touch and drew 'people's princess' headlines.

Zara is Spanish-owned, so while Kate's love for the label might not be a demonstration of support for a British business, it's a way for her to show that she's just like the rest of us. Many of Kate's skinny jeans are from Zara and she has favoured its tailored blazers for dressing up those jeans. She chooses it for more formal events, too; a crystal necklace that she wore on the red carpet in 2015 and a headband for the Festival of Remembrance in 2019 both came from the chain.

As Kate's style has evolved, her dedication to Zara has been unfaltering, but her purchases are more carefully judged. She now prefers its midi dresses with fashionable flourishes, like balloon sleeves or a pussy-bow neckline, and directional designs like culottes or acid-hued knitwear. Kate doesn't only shop for herself at Zara; she's been seen with bags from Zara Home and Princess Charlotte has worn a dress from the Kids section.

*Kate's Zara wardrobe:*

| | |
|---|---|
| 10 dresses | 10 trousers |
| 22 coats and | 2 skirts |
| jackets | 1 necklace |
| 6 tops | 1 hairband |

**RIGHT** Kate and William leaving Buckingham Palace the day after their wedding with Kate in a cornflower blue Zara dress and L.K. Bennett patent wedge heels.

# KATE'S MATERNITY STYLE

Few women would envy the Duchess of Cambridge having to dress a growing bump in the public eye. Although she suffered with severe morning sickness in the first months of her pregnancies, Kate undertook charity visits, foreign tours and royal duties while she was expecting, learning to tweak her signature style to accommodate her changing shape. In doing so, she wielded some of the most impactful fashion influence of her royal life.

The Duchess stuck to her tried-and-tested method of mixing bespoke, designer looks with affordable buys while she was pregnant, so for every Emilia Wickstead dress or Catherine Walker & Co coat, there was an ASOS or Topshop dress that any other expectant mum could snap up.

Not that Kate always stuck strictly to maternity wear. One of the biggest stories of Kate Effect frenzy to emerge during her first pregnancy in 2013 was that she'd picked up a £37 floral dress from Lovestruck, a concession in Topshop. With its elasticated waistband, the design was an excellent example of the growing trend for pregnant women to buy pieces from 'normal' ranges that would work with their changing bodies. She might never have been seen wearing the dress publicly, but it still sold out and prompted visits to the brand's website to soar from 500 to 60,000 a day after Topshop tipped off the media about Kate's purchase.

Topshop was a particular favourite when Kate was expecting Prince George, and she added two other pregnancy-friendly designs to her collection: a 1960s-style shift with Peter Pan collar and a £38 polka dot Empire-line dress that she wore for a visit to the Harry Potter studios, which sold out soon after she wore it. Another polka dot hit came when the Duchess was pregnant with Princess Charlotte; the wrap dress from ASOS's maternity line was out of stock within 30 minutes of pictures of the Duchess wearing it hitting the internet.

When Kate did choose maternity-specific pieces, her most-loved label was Seraphine, whose tag line is 'fashionably pregnant'. Known for its elegant aesthetic, the brand's look seemed a perfect fit with the Duchess's personal style. She first gave Seraphine a taste of the Kate Effect when she wore its knot front maternity dress in pictures taken at her parents' home in Bucklebury when Prince George was a few weeks old. In a sign of a refreshingly down-to-earth attitude, Kate was relaxed about being photographed in a maternity dress post-birth, which perhaps contributed to a sudden spike in interest in the label. 'Suddenly the whole world was talking about Seraphine. Of course, the dress sold out in a matter of hours and we had to create a waiting list,' remembers Cécile Reinaud, Seraphine's founder. 'This was a real turning point – our international following grew enormously overnight.'

When she was expecting Princess Charlotte, the Duchess gave Seraphine another boost by wearing its tweed coat on a visit to New York (see page 38). 'This was a huge moment for us in terms of brand awareness in the US,' Reinaud explains. 'We had just opened our first flagship store in New York, so the timing couldn't have been better.'

**OPPOSITE** Harry, Kate and William on the Harry Potter set at the Warner Bros studio in Hertfordshire, April 2013. Kate teamed her polka dot dress from Topshop with a black Ralph Lauren blazer.

**LEFT** The Duke and Duchess of Cambridge on the first day of a trip to New York in December 2014. Kate opted for a coat by British brand Seraphine.

**OPPOSITE** On a royal tour of India in April 2016, Kate wore a maxi dress by Glamorous to visit a charity supporting street children.

# IS IT RIGHT TO WEAR HIGH STREET?

A royal tour comes with a tangled web of fashion requirements, and one of Kate's trickiest challenges yet was a visit to homeless children in New Delhi during a tour to India in 2016. The children were expecting a princess, but where once it might have seemed acceptable for a royal to make such a visit wearing classically regal clothing, that would now feel off-message for Kate and William, keen to present a more relaxed, informal image of the monarchy.

So the Duchess's £50 dress from Manchester-based high-street label Glamorous at first seemed like a great choice. Worn with flat sandals, its length and long sleeves made it appropriately modest and it shone a light on British business – Glamorous reported that the dress quickly sold out, with 1,000 customers a minute looking at the dress online when pictures of Kate were released.

However, the ethics of wearing a fast fashion label in a country where sweatshop labour conditions are a harsh everyday reality was quickly called into question. Kate's dress, Glamorous said, had been made in China, but they did work with factories in India. And what about the fact that the dress's print imitated traditional Indian textiles but had not actually benefitted anyone in India? It was a similar scenario with another Indian-looking design from Topshop that Kate wore later in the visit.

The price tags and nods to the British high street played well, but the deeper issues that the look raised proved that a dress is never just a dress. It was telling that visiting Pakistan three years later, Kate wore Pakistani designers almost exclusively.

**OPPOSITE** Reiss repeats. Kate wearing the brand's white Olivia coat in 2020 (main picture) and, from top to bottom, in 2009, 2008 and 2007.

# KATE the great recycler

One of the Duchess of Cambridge's favoured strategies has been to 'recycle' outfits. Logic might suggest that a look loses its appeal second time around, but when Kate recycles she is praised for her thrift, ability to fit into something a decade old, and downplaying her appearance.

Like high-street shopping, repeating is the Duchess's way of portraying how down to earth she is, and that despite owning wardrobes of bespoke designer creations, she, too, has old favourites – even if in reality we can count the number of public wears on one hand.

So what are the recycles that really thrill? Anything that had major impact the first time around is guaranteed to be a nostalgia-evoking hit the second time; when Kate attended a gala dinner at Houghton Hall in Norfolk in 2016, she revived the Jenny Packham gown she'd worn for her first big black tie outing as a royal in 2011, and in 2019 she arrived at the Commonwealth Day Service at Westminster Abbey in a Catherine Walker & Co double-breasted coat dress first seen in New Zealand in 2014.

Then there are the re-wears that ignite a mystery. When the Duchess apparently re-wore a floral McQueen gown to a National Portrait Gallery gala in 2019, it appeared she had tweaked her look from the 2017 BAFTAs to have shoulder-covering sleeves, but a little sleuthing showed that the pattern placement was different, so was it in fact two similar but distinct pieces? Perhaps Kate had taken inspiration from the Queen and Princess Anne, who have been known to use existing material to make new items so it doesn't go to waste? Even if it was new, the dress read as a coffer-friendly recycle in most of the coverage.

But by far the most potent re-wear ploy is when the Duchess is seen in the same pieces time and again, ideally over a number of years. These are her forever favourites...

# THE REISS COAT

A wardrobe surprise came during the Duke and Duchess of Cambridge's visit to Ireland in March 2020 when Kate donned Reiss's Olivia coat, a style that had been part of her wardrobe during her royal girlfriend days (see page 41). Most would have assumed it had been sent to the charity shop, but Kate proved her eco credentials by having the coat tailored to a sleeker fit. 'It was great to see Kate re-wear the Olivia coat,' says Reiss CEO Christos Angelides of the coat, which Kate was first pictured wearing in November 2007. Its most significant outing came in April 2008, when Kate was pictured with William at his RAF wings graduation ceremony.

# THE LUISA SPAGNOLI SUIT

One of Kate's most famous post-engagement looks was a scarlet skirt suit by Italian label Luisa Spagnoli, which she wore to visit St Andrews – her and William's alma mater – a couple of months before their marriage. If at the time it seemed a tad staid for a radiant new princess, it has turned out to be one of the hardest-working looks in her royal wardrobe. It's enjoyed four outings, and has been worn for everything from a game of cricket to the Queen's Christmas lunch. One subtle alteration was made to render the suit truly duchess-worthy; the original dress was remade into a longer knee-length skirt.

**ABOVE LEFT AND LEFT** Kate's Luisa Spagnoli suit worn on a trip to Christchurch, New Zealand in April 2014 (above left). The suit's first outing was back in 2011, when Kate chose it for a pre-wedding visit to the University of St Andrews with Prince William (left).

# THE PENELOPE CHILVERS BOOTS

The longest-surviving items in the Duchess of Cambridge's repertoire are her Penelope Chilvers Tassel riding boots, which she was first pictured wearing in 2004. Since then, they've taken her trekking in Bhutan, to a traditional ceremony performed by the Heiltsuk people in British Columbia and to a farm in Northern Ireland, with Kate totting up at least eight public wears of the boots.

'While living in Barcelona I used to enjoy riding in my lunch break, in the hills above the city,' says Chilvers of the boots' origins. 'I was on the lookout for the perfect riding boots and tracked down an artisan bootmaker to make me a pair to my own measurements and design. When I came back to live in London, all my friends wanted some, too. This is how my business began.'

Chilvers, who first met Kate and her mother at a Christmas fair in the early days of her business, believes that the Duchess has been wearing the same pair of boots for 16 years, 'making a true testament to their timeless appeal and longevity'.

'Sales soar each time she wears Penelope Chilvers, with orders flooding in from all over the world. And our reputation for well-made, long-lasting products is something that stems from her inimitable style. It's something we vouch to cherish and preserve. I will forever be so grateful to her.'

**ABOVE RIGHT AND RIGHT** The first sighting of Kate's Penelope Chilvers Tassel riding boots was in 2004 at a game fair at Blenheim Palace (above right). More recently, she reached for them for a visit to an open farm on a trip to Northern Ireland in February 2020 (right).

# KATE on tour

The art of packing for a royal tour is unimaginably complex. These are
megawatt moments, especially for the Duke and Duchess of Cambridge,
who are the British Royal Family's glamorous young stars. Where they go,
the world's media follow – on their first tour as a married couple in 2011,
1,300 journalists were accredited to cover the trip.

Not only does a tour create a snap of interest in the country the couple visit, but they are commented upon globally. Get it right, and this is a priceless PR and diplomacy opportunity.

These intense bursts of activity are reflected in the wardrobe requirements. During her first tour, Kate wore 20 outfits over 11 days, ranging from canoeing gear to evening gowns. Careful thought is required to ensure every ensemble sends the right message, conforms to local customs, will photograph nicely from even the trickiest angles (alighting aeroplanes is a particular challenge) and can stand up to all weathers. So, besides the outfits we actually see, it's likely that there are plenty of back-ups that never see the light of day.

We can get some idea of the Duchess's packing list from an inventory of Princess Diana's luggage for one of her tours in 1985: 20 daytime looks, 12 hats, more than 12 evening dresses, 15 matching shoes and bags, 19 pairs of earrings, two tiaras and eight necklaces. Kate's team has been photographed hauling hatboxes, trunks, suitcases and garment bags from the plane during foreign visits. There is certainly no such thing as travelling light when it comes to tour wardrobes.

Kate's approach might be more informal than Diana's, because times, and therefore expectations, have changed, but the pressure is on in a different way. Each of her outfits is dissected the moment she steps out and every small detail is captured and read into. This has created chances to push the boundaries of soft power dressing, but there is no space for slip-ups.

Almost every day of a tour offers picture opportunities that are maximized through the medium of fashion. There's a selection of tactics that Kate uses to make her clothing amplify the impression she wishes to make, and she ticks off each category at salient moments on each visit.

credentials and bringing the Commonwealth country in on the romantic fairytale of her and William's relationship.

Another priority is showcasing British fashion. As one of the industry's most influential ambassadors, the Duchess has made household names of the British designers that she has worn abroad, offering a boost to their businesses and reputation. One of the most sensitive examples of this was a paisley Alexander McQueen dress that Kate wore in India – not only was the frock an example of great British design, but also the teardrop pattern represented the ties between the two countries. Originally woven in the Kashmir region in the 11th century and eventually arriving in the United Kingdom via the East India Company in the 1700s, it became known as Paisley after the Scottish town that later began to produce sought-after scarves and fabrics in the swirling print. It was deft, too, that in New Zealand the Duchess wore a bespoke dress by Emilia Wickstead, who grew up in the country but is now a star of London Fashion Week.

The most potent option at the Duchess's disposal is fashion diplomacy, wearing looks by local designers and paying respect to the customs of the country she is visiting. These outfits are not always immediately obvious, but once we are told who it is designed by, those names can expect new global renown – it's the height of fashion flattery.

More instantaneous is when Kate adopts traditional garments, as she did in Pakistan and Bhutan, when her look is respectful of her destination (she always incorporates scarves that

The Duchess will always want to underscore her relatability, so we can expect a high-street purchase or re-wear at some point, but this can still be tailored to the occasion – in Australia in 2014, she opted for a soft beige and cappuccino checked Hobbs dress to pose in front of the arid, earthy landscape of Uluru, complementing her backdrop meticulously. Meanwhile, in Canada in 2011, Kate re-wore the Reiss dress she'd debuted in her engagement portraits, simultaneously reminding the world of her bargain-scouting can be used to cover her head at a mosque), or when she dresses in a nation's signature colours or prints, like the red and white combinations she chose in Canada or the Emerald Isle-green items worn in Ireland. This is an approach that has evolved over time; in India in 2016, the Duchess chose lots of Indian-looking pieces from US and British labels, but by the time she went to Pakistan in 2019, she'd refined her approach and shopped from Pakistani designers, wearing authentic pieces created and designed in the country.

Once the clothing choices are made, careful preparation and attention to detail is required to ensure that Kate – and her clothes – are ready to face the cameras. In the early days, she hadn't learned the Queen's trick of weighting her hems to ensure that skirts didn't blow up in a gust of wind, but now weather-proofing tweaks will be taken into account, as well as modifications to make items suitably demure, like extra linings or panels.

Meghan, the Duchess of Sussex, forgot to remove the label from her Self-Portrait dress when she arrived in Tonga in 2018, prompting an unfortunate slew of headlines. Kate has never made such a slip-up, which is credit to the care taken by her personal assistant Natasha Archer, who masterminds the Duchess's tour wardrobes and accompanies her on trips to make sure the end result is impeccable.

Another vital member of the entourage is hairdresser Amanda Cook Tucker, who is tasked with keeping the Duchess's brunette hair glossy and bouncy at all times, whether she's in tropical humidity or sub-zero winds, dining with fellow royalty or competing in a cricket match. Before a visit to Sweden and Norway in 2018, Cook Tucker revealed the full kit required for a week on the road with Kate. Her Instagram account was

hastily deleted after the post went viral, which is a lesson in the intention of a royal tour; months of work and preparation go into ensuring everything goes perfectly, but the ultimate effect should be effortless and seamlessly polished.

## Countries Kate has visited:

Canada (twice), the US (twice), Denmark, Singapore, Malaysia, the Solomon Islands, Tuvalu, New Zealand, Australia, France, Belgium, India, Bhutan, the Netherlands, Luxembourg, Poland, Germany, Sweden, Norway, Cyprus, Pakistan and Ireland.

## Number of looks worn:

Canada and the US 2011: *20 looks in 11 days*

Singapore, Malaysia, the Solomon Islands and Tuvalu 2012: *16 looks in 8 days*

New Zealand and Australia 2014: *23 looks in 18 days*

India and Bhutan 2016: *18 looks in 6 days*

Canada 2016: *14 looks in 7 days*

Poland and Germany 2017: *9 looks in 5 days*

Sweden and Norway 2018: *9 looks in 4 days*

Pakistan 2019: *10 looks in 5 days*

Ireland 2020: *7 looks in 3 days*

**LEFT** The Duke and Duchess of Cambridge disembark the HMCS Montreal after arriving in Quebec City in 2011. Kate wears Erdem.

**OPPOSITE** Kate dons a Prabal Gurung shift dress to meet the President of Singapore and his wife, September 2012.

# CANADA, 2011

Kate and William's visit to Canada and the US just months after their wedding was a blockbuster event, a chance to launch the Royal Family's new power duo on the world stage. The Duchess's fashion was vital during the visit; modern, fresh choices would emphasize the excitement of the new generation, while interweaving traditional signs of respect and diplomacy created the continuity upon which the monarchy depends.

The Erdem sleek shift dress that the Duchess picked to wear on a stop in Quebec was emblematic of how Kate was melding these competing demands. Designer Erdem Moralioglu was born in Montreal, Quebec but had moved to London to study fashion and was now one of London Fashion Week's star names; meanwhile, the lace-detailed dress was the same rich royal blue as the region's flag.

# SINGAPORE, 2012

If the Duchess was a little tentative about fashion in her early royal years, then the Prabal Gurung dress that she wore on the first day of a tour celebrating the Queen's Diamond Jubilee, starting in Singapore, was a joy to behold.

Kate stepped out of her comfort zone for an official welcome reception hosted by the President of Singapore in a sleek silk shift dress emblazoned with an opulent purple botanical print inspired by

Japanese photographer Nobuyoshi Araki's Sensual Flowers series – an appropriate reference, given that the royal couple had just had an orchid named in their honour.

Though Gurung was forging a reputation as one of New York's most exciting labels, he was born in Singapore in the early 1970s. Thus, the Duchess's dress was also a show of support for one of her host's promising creative exports.

# SOLOMON ISLANDS, 2012

The Duchess has rarely put a foot wrong when it comes to diplomatic fashion gestures. But she did make an unintentional mistake during a visit to the Solomon Islands in 2012. Described as everything from a 'gaffe' to a 'scandal' in the press, the episode was an apt lesson in the embarrassment that a style misstep can create.

For an evening reception during their visit to Honiara, the islands' capital, Kate and William wore a shirt and a dress that had been left in her hotel room. Despite not resembling the outfits they thought they were being given to wear, they donned them anyway after being assured they had been made locally.

However, it later emerged that an over-enthusiastic government official had laid out extra gifts, and that Kate's pink tiered dress was in fact made by a label called Tav and gifted by Ellena Tavioni, a boutique owner from the Cook Islands 3,000 miles away.

The Cambridges' representatives were forced to release a statement explaining what had happened:

'We saw they weren't the same design of the traditional clothes we were told would be gifted. So we checked with the Solomon Islands government to ensure the right ones were worn. We were reassured the clothes were correct, and so the Duke and Duchess wore them to the event. It was not learned until later in the evening that the clothes weren't from the islands. But it was understood that the Duke and Duchess intended to wear traditional Solomon Island clothes and this was appreciated. No offence was caused.'

The faux pas was a lesson in the perils of fashion gestures going wrong. Someone was happy, though. 'The more I look at the picture, the more I think it was just perfect for her,' Tavioni told *The New Zealand Herald*. 'When I saw them wearing it, I felt a bit humbled that they were wearing something that was made in the Pacific and that it was good enough for them to wear.'

**OPPOSITE** The Duke and Duchess of Cambridge don what were believed to be locally made outfits for an evening reception on a trip to the Solomon Islands in 2012.

**RIGHT** For the couple's 2014 visit to Manly Beach in Sydney, Kate opted for a cream broderie anglaise dress by Zimmermann.

# AUSTRALIA, 2014

A day at the beach is a quintessential Australian activity, so it was no surprise that a visit to a surf camp was scheduled into Kate and William's itinerary during their 2014 tour. But how to remain appropriate and elegant in a scenario where most people wear a t-shirt and shorts?

The Australian label Zimmermann was conceived almost exactly for this dilemma,

crafting pretty, bohemian-luxe dresses that are favourites among the celebrity and socialite set. The Duchess used her beach moment to give Zimmermann the royal seal of approval, wearing its crisp broderie anglaise Roamer dress at Sydney's Manly Beach. It was refined enough to work for the rest of the day's activities, too – a visit to an Easter show and a children's hospice.

# INDIA, 2016

On the first day of the Duke and Duchess's tour to India in 2016, Kate reinforced her personal take on diplomatic dressing by opting for a dress by Mumbai-based designer Anita Dongre that she had altered to suit a schedule that included a cricket match with Sachin Tendulkar.

Dongre only found out that the Duchess was wearing her design 'when social media went ballistic. The global press were calling up, customers wanted to buy the dress; all those responses were overwhelming.' Dongre's website even crashed, such was the interest sparked by Kate's patronage.

Natasha Archer had adapted the pink and green dress – which had been shown on the catwalk at Lakme Fashion Week as a long-length tunic with matching trousers and scarf – with her own injection of creativity. 'In India, we wear kurtas, which are like tunics. That's how it was shown on my website,' Dongre explains. 'Natasha ordered the tunic and stole, then cut the stole up to make a belt. I liked the way that Natasha belted it. I thought that was really cool.'

Almost a year after Kate wore Dongre's dress in India, the designer was invited to the UK to attend a reception celebrating the UK-India year of culture where she was able to meet the Duchess in person. 'We had a really long conversation and I fell in love with her,' Dongre recalls. 'She knew a lot about my work and designs. I was quite amazed at how knowledgeable she was about what I do.'

# BHUTAN, 2016

A tour is often just as much about who the royals might meet as where they will go. When it was announced that the Cambridges would be dropping into the tiny kingdom of Bhutan as part of their 2016 tour to India, there was great excitement that Kate Middleton would get to meet 'the Kate Middleton of the Himalayas', Bhutan's beautiful, stylish young Queen Jetsun Pema (see page 46).

In an act of masterful sartorial respect, the Duchess wore a traditional Bhutanese outfit to meet the Queen. The centrepiece of the look was a 'half-kira' skirt, which had been made for Kate in London from fabric woven by hand in Bhutan using traditional techniques. The purple fabric used for Kate's look was created by Kelzang Wangmo, a favourite weaver of the Bhutanese Royal Family, and her team.

In a rare decision to publicize the Duchess's fashion choices on its own social media channels, Kensington Palace posted a video on Twitter showing Mrs Wangmo's reaction when they told her that her fabric had been used to create Kate's half-kira. 'I'm so happy the Duchess is wearing a piece from my shop,' she says, beaming.

Finishing the look with an intricately embroidered Lyrisme cape from French brand Paul & Joe and L.K. Bennett heels, Kate epitomized diplomatic sophistication as she walked alongside Queen Jetsun Pema, wearing her own bright red, opulently embroidered kira, at the welcome ceremony.

**OPPOSITE** On a trip to India in 2016 in a dress by Mumbai-based designer Anita Dongre.

# PARIS, 2017

It would have been the ultimate missed fashion opportunity had the Duchess of Cambridge not worn Dior or Chanel during a visit to Paris, the home of haute couture, in March 2017 (see page 44). It might usually be tricky for a future British queen to justify wearing French designers, but a spot of fashion flattery was the perfect excuse.

Both fashion houses had a history of dressing royalty. The Queen Mother and Princess Margaret were fans of Dior, with Margaret wearing one of the couturier's creations for her 21st birthday. Diana turned to Chanel for a visit to Paris in 1988, and wore the label's skirt suits as her style became more streamlined in the 1990s.

Kate opted to wear Chanel for a morning at Les Invalides and the Musée d'Orsay. Her black tweed coat dress was cinched at the waist with a CC logo belt and accessorized with a burgundy Chanel handbag. The Duchess underscored the diplomacy point by adding jewellery by Cartier. Not only did the outfit meet with approval from the hard-to-please French press, it also elevated Kate's fashion kudos.

# POLAND, 2017

The Duchess of Cambridge's most experimental diplomatic fashion moment came at a garden party in Warsaw in July 2017. It's fair to say that Poland does not come with the same style template and expectations as a visit to India or Paris, where saris and Chanel respectively spring to mind. But for the tour's only evening engagement, Kate wore a pristine white silk dress with jagged architectural pleats and delicate detailing by Polish designer Gosia Baczyńska.

Natasha Archer emailed Baczyńska a month before the trip requesting a lookbook. The message launched the designer into a creative spin, and she sent lots of ideas to Archer. Sensitive to the royal standards of modesty, Baczyńska offered to remake pieces in longer lengths or with sleeves; when she sent a picture of the dress that the Duchess would eventually wear, she wrote: 'off-white, a bit edgy but still elegant – I can make an interpretation of this style (for e.g. sleeves)'.

Once she had sent a few options to London, all Baczyńska could do was wait. She had been invited to the garden party, in celebration of the Queen's 90th birthday, at Warsaw's Orangery, and saw the Duchess arrive wearing her dress. 'I was extremely happy… That was like a dream,' she remembers. Baczyńska was able to meet the Duchess that night. 'We spoke for a while. Kate was surprised to meet me, so it was funny but very, very nice.'

OPPOSITE Kate wears a white silk dress by Polish designer Gosia Baczyńska to a celebration of the Queen's 90th birthday at the Orangery, Warsaw in July 2017.

RIGHT The Duke and Duchess of Cambridge with Crown Prince Haakon and Crown Princess Mette-Marit on a visit to Norway in 2018. Kate's jacket is by Norwegian skiwear label KJUS.

# NORWAY, 2018

One of the most powerful – and blatant– ways to deploy fashion as a tool for soft power is to dress as the flag of your hosts. Princess Diana exhibited this tactic in Japan, where her red spotted dress, picked up at a boutique in Fulham, echoed the rising sun motif seen on the country's flag.

The Duchess of Cambridge offered her own sporty spin on flag dressing in February 2018, when she donned a jacket by KJUS, a ski label founded by Norwegian ski champion Lasse Kjus, for a visit to the Holmenkollen ski jump with Crown Prince Haakon and Crown Princess Mette-Marit of Norway, during a royal tour to Scandinavia. Kate's jacket was bright red with white stripes, only missing a flash of blue to make it a complete homage to the Norwegian flag. Layered underneath Kate's jacket was a cosy sweater from another local label, Dale of Norway, which had been a gift from the King and Queen of Norway.

This show of diplomacy was enhanced later in the visit when Kate posed with a group of children all dressed in red and waving Norwegian flags.

# The making of Kate's Pakistan 'tourdrobe', 2019

When the Cambridges visited Pakistan in October 2019, the visit was hailed as a masterclass in diplomacy. Kate and William struck the perfect balance of regal and normal, as easy-going playing at tea parties with a little girl in a cancer hospital as they were composed and thoughtful taking part in prayers at Badshahi Mosque in Lahore.

A vital element in the tour's success was the Duchess's ultra-respectful wardrobe. It was the first time that she had overhauled her personal style for a foreign visit, putting together a selection of looks that paid homage to the traditions of Pakistani dress and celebrating them afresh.

If the Duchess looked calmly elegant in her selection of cream, jade green and blue Pakistani purchases, then she belied the flurry of activity that had taken place in the weeks before the tour to ensure that each detail was perfect.

Back in London in mid-September, Onita Prasada – a specialist in Asian couture – had arrived at her boutique, O'nitaa in Chelsea, expecting a normal day. Had she checked her emails from the previous evening, she'd have known that Natasha Archer, the Duchess's personal assistant, had put in a request for help.

'I think she googled us and found out that we were one of the stores that stocked Pakistani merchandise in the vicinity,' Prasada remembers. 'I walked into the store and she was there… I talked her through every item that we have in the store, including the accessories and jewellery. I talked to her about how we think as Asians and how we dress as Asians.' With the Royal Family always intent on not putting a foot wrong and respecting local customs, Archer soaked up all the wisdom and knowledge that Prasada had to offer.

Although Archer was adamant that 'the Duchess has her own identity and we mustn't keep trying to compare her with Diana', Prasada couldn't help but be inspired by the fashion choices that Prince William's mother had made on her visits to Pakistan in the 1990s.

Another consideration was ensuring that there was no potential for controversy with Kate's clothing. 'We were very, very particular that everything came from Pakistan and not mixing India anywhere in the vicinity,' says Prasada. 'I think that was out of respect for the Pakistani community.' Given the fractious history of Indian-Pakistani relations, any missteps could have had unfortunate repercussions.

At the end of her visit, Archer packed a number of samples into her car to take back and show the Duchess. There followed a few weeks of back and forth between Prasada and the palace as they settled on the designers that Kate would wear.

They eventually chose Maheen Khan, a designer who has been dubbed Pakistan's answer to Coco Chanel thanks to her sophisticated aesthetic. Fittingly, Khan had also worked with Catherine Walker & Co in the past, the same Chelsea couturier that provided two looks for the Duchess's tour wardrobe.

'The lines of Maheen's garments are very simple; they're classic and she's minimalistic with her embellishments,' Prasada elaborates. 'When you're living in a country and being influenced by the environment, your tendency is to sway more to ethnic convention. Maheen breaks out of that. She's more European in her styling, but she brings in the colours and the cuts, and understands the figure – it's beautiful.'

**RIGHT** Kate wore a blue kurta by designer Maheen Khan to visit a school in Islamabad on the Duke and Duchess's 2019 Pakistan tour.

While the Duchess's tour wardrobe was coming together nicely, Prasada was on another mission: to persuade Prince William to join in with the diplomatic dressing. 'Every time Natasha picked up something, I told her we would have something that could complement this garment if the Duke dressed in this. But she explained that the Duke never wears anything that's not from his own wardrobe. Being very proud of being an Asian, I thought, "Why not? I don't think you know how beautiful our men's style is." I followed with photographs, and as luck would have it, she called me and said, "You know all those images that you shared with me? The Duke is toying with the idea of wearing a local outfit for one of the occasions." That was absolutely fabulous.'

Prasada's encouragement did not stop there, as she worked to convince the Prince, via Natasha, that the pieces he had decided on were a little too simple for the gala reception at which they would be worn.

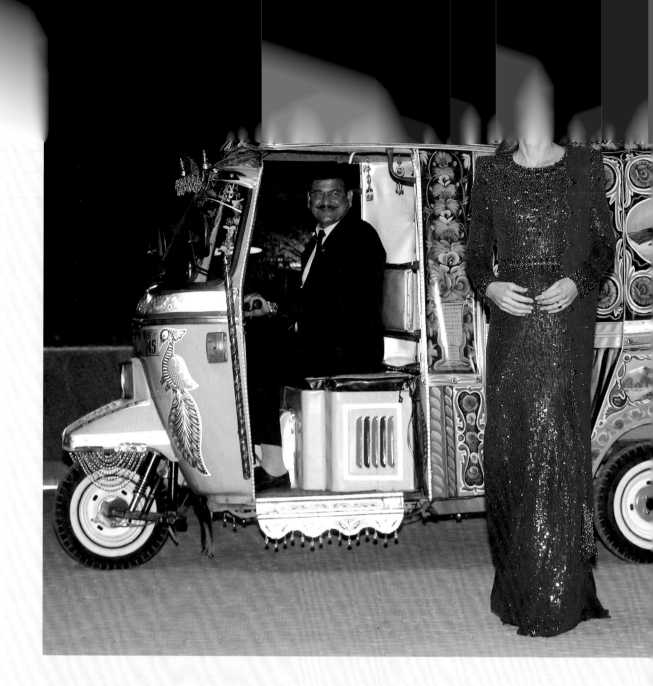

After letting Nauman Arfeen, the menswear designer William had selected to wear, in on the secret so that he would create the required looks with just 48 hours turnaround, Prasada still wasn't happy. She enlisted Arfeen to make a more formal version of the green sherwani that had been requested, in keeping with the royal preference to dress to match their host country's flag. When it arrived in London, Prasada dispatched her most trusted tailor to the palace to ensure that Wiliam's outfit was an immaculate fit.

'We ended up having the joy of seeing the Duke in this absolutely magnificent jacket. It ended up picking up a lot of press and for the

first time ever he upstaged the Duchess,' Prasada remembers, overjoyed at the memory of her role in William's first go at diplomatic dressing. On the evening that William wore his sherwani, Kate looked glamorous in a deep green gown by Jenny Packham with a coordinating dupatta scarf and opulent earrings from O'nitaa.

Kate made headlines around the world for her Pakistan look. On social media, Pakistani women praised her demure yet fashionable style. 'Thanks for promoting the real and positive image of Pakistan,' said one user.

Kate's Maheen Khan outfits included a periwinkle blue kurta for a school visit and a turquoise and gold shalwar kameez for an afternoon of visits in Lahore. Both pieces included panels of embroidery around the neckline, a traditional technique called *phulkari*. Besides Khan, the Duchess incorporated affordable items from Pakistani retailers, such as jewellery from Zeen, a scarf from Satrangi and kurtas by Gul Ahmed and Élan.

'A modern Pakistani would dress like that,' acknowledges Prasada, who sent photographs and videos to Archer advising her on how outfits should be styled and scarves draped.

'I would applaud the fact that she made the effort to respect the traditional dress code. And her personality shone through.'

The Duchess's respectful dressing continued once she was home. Not only did she re-wear her Zeen earrings for a day in Bradford, where she visited a Pakistani restaurant, but she wrote to the designers who had helped her pull off her tour de force. 'I am so grateful to you and your team for designing such a wonderful selection to choose from – although having so many beautiful things did make decision making a little more difficult!' Kate wrote to Khan. 'I really enjoyed wearing both your outfits – and the trousers were such a great fit, too.'

Prasada's part in the Cambridges' cleverest show of fashion diplomacy yet has given a global boost to her business. 'A very large percentage of our client base flies in from America,' she says. 'Since the Cambridge episode, I think it's quadrupled. And there has been huge interest from Australia, Germany and Spain, too.' Proof that a carefully considered tour wardrobe can wield influence far beyond the country it's conceived to flatter.

**OPPOSITE** The Duchess
chose Erdem for a visit to
the RHS Chelsea Flower
Show in May 2019 with
the Queen and the Duke
of Cambridge.

# harnessing the
# POWER OF FASHION

'I have to be seen to be believed,' the Queen once said, summing up
in those eight words the necessary spectacle of royalty. Yes, there are
speeches, conversations and small talk involved in the job, but all that
would count for little without a carefully crafted image; a moment of
visual magic that conjures instant mystique.

The Queen does it with her bright, matching
hats and coats and a boxy Launer handbag as
a constant companion. The rest of her family have
their own signifiers. It's no accident that Prince
Charles relies on Savile Row suits, always worn
with a dapper detail such as a floral buttonhole or
pocket square, or that Princess Anne's immovable
hairsprayed chignon is never out of place.

Beyond making a royal recognizable from
(almost) a mile off, a thoughtfully selected
wardrobe imbues added meaning and significance
to an engagement. An outfit might not be
anything to do with the visit itself, but rather a
message they wish to convey on that day, like the
Queen's decision to wear green on the anniversary
of the Grenfell Tower fire, a shade that had
become a symbol of hope and solidarity in the
aftermath of the disaster.

The Duchess of Cambridge has evidently
embarked on her own study of the Queen's
sartorial ways and how she might interpret
them as she moulds her own image. A glance at
Princess Diana's modus operandi will also have
helped Kate. Diana realized more than anyone
how the right outfit at the right time could speak
a thousand words. The Duchess is unlikely to wish
to craft the same reputation as a clothes horse,
but she has melded that knack for creating marvel
with the Queen's stoic sense of sartorial duty to
arrive at her own version of royal fashion power.

From the beginning, Kate has adopted a
'literal dressing' strategy. Just as royals are
accorded the respect of a posy of flowers and
a curtsey or a bow by those that they visit, so the
Duchess offers her own tribute by dressing to
match her destination and tells us the purpose

of her day simply through the choice of the right dress or colour. But it's all about striking a balance, and although dressing to a theme is important, the look should never err into fancy-dress territory.

If Kate is in stripes, there's probably a nautical link. Florals for flower shows? That's prime, if not exactly groundbreaking, Duchess-dressing territory. You won't be surprised to learn that Kate's favoured shade for a visit to Wimbledon is tennis whites white, or that she loves to wear festive tartan at Christmas.

While 'the more obvious the better' is the Duchess's favoured course of fashion action, there are times when her choices require translation. The significance can come in the label she has opted to wear or more subtle signals. At a gala event to open the Natural History Museum's Blue Whale exhibit, Kate chose Prada sandals with wave-like straps, and when visiting Bletchley Park, home of the Second World War's codebreakers, she chose a 1940s-style Alessandra Rich dress from a collection inspired by the famous 'Sailor Kiss' photograph taken on VJ day.

This is a style formula that many of us reach for subconsciously in our everyday lives and which governs so many cultural rituals. It's useful to compare Kate's task when she gets dressed each day with how we might prepare for a wedding: checking our outfit will photograph well, suits the event and evokes the meaning we desire.

The difference for the Duchess is that the stakes are not merely personal. Hers is a uniform responsible for fostering admiration for the Royal Family and slowly introducing the idea of herself and her husband as The Firm's next generation of leaders. It's a tall order, but in this unenviable style challenge, Kate rarely puts a foot wrong.

# AS A COWGIRL AT THE CALGARY STAMPEDE, 2011

Kate mastered dressing for the most unexpected of occasions early on in her royal life, wearing one of her best literal looks just a few months after her marriage during the couple's first tour together in Canada. They spent the day at the Calgary Stampede, a bucking bronco-tastic showcase of Western tradition that calls itself 'the greatest outdoor show on earth'.

William and Kate embraced the rodeo dress code, sporting jeans, cowboy boots and the crème de la crème of stetsons, the 'official white hat' created by Canadian label Smithbilt and crafted from rabbit fur felt.

While the Duchess certainly looked the part in her pretty embroidered Alice Temperley blouse and flared jeans, she chose not to wear the cowboy boots made for her by the Alberta Boot Company, instead showcasing a pair of boots by London label R.Soles, which specializes in authentic Western-style boots.

That the Cambridges embraced stampede style is evidence of their determination to be accessible and informal; when the Queen attended the same event in 1959, she remained in her floral sun dress, elegant hat and white gloves – although Prince Philip did don a stetson.

**OPPOSITE** The Duke and Duchess of Cambridge at the Calgary Stampede, July 2011, wearing stetsons by Smithbilt Hats.

# IN GREEN AT THE NATURAL HISTORY MUSEUM, 2012

You might not expect a politically neutral Duchess to adopt the peace sign, but it was perhaps the other motif – a leafy tree – that appeared on an emerald green silk tea dress by Mulberry that appealed to Kate.

This was one of the more fashion-forward choices she made in the early years of royal life. The 1970s-style dress, with its homage to nature, worked perfectly for the opening of the new Treasures gallery at the Natural History Museum in November 2012.

This look ultimately became doubly meaningful. That evening, Kate also unveiled a new fringe/bangs. Many wondered what the transformation might mean, given that women often change their hair at significant milestones in their lives. 'I'd love to say I talked her into it,' reveals Richard Ward, her hairdresser, 'but she just phoned me up one day and said I want you to cut a fringe – when can you come over and do it?' A few days later, it was announced that the Duchess was pregnant with her first baby. Now, whenever she changes her hair, it prompts a flurry of speculation.

**LEFT** Kate in Mulberry at the Natural History Museum, November 2012.

**OPPOSITE** Wearing Alexander McQueen for a visit to a sailing charity in Portsmouth, May 2016.

# NAUTICAL IN PORTSMOUTH, 2016

The Duchess of Cambridge has made stripes, the combination of navy and white and naval detailing a style signature. And that's mostly thanks to her close association with sailing, which began with her support for Team GB's sailing squad at the London 2012 Olympics and culminated with her and William's reviving the King's Cup Regatta in 2019 as an annual fundraising effort.

In May 2016, Kate donned her very best sailor style for a visit to the Portsmouth headquarters of Olympic sailor Sir Ben Ainslie's 1851 Trust, which seeks to inspire young people to try sailing. This was the third outing for Kate's blouse and pencil skirt ensemble by Alexander McQueen, but its sailor-style gold buttons and frogging finishes meant it was the ideal nautical-themed choice. Later in the day, Kate changed into a pair of Adidas trainers and sailing gear to get stuck into the activities – proof of the remarkable versatility required of her wardrobe.

# LE KILT IN SCOTLAND, 2016

Given London's community of young designers, some found it surprising that the Duchess was tentative in buying from these labels, for whom a show of royal support could be transformative. Preferring to take a considered approach to her royal wardrobe, Kate has selected just a few names – like Emilia Wickstead and Erdem – whose aesthetic chimes closely with her own. But when the occasion is right, Kate can be more adventurous.

On a visit to Edinburgh in 2016, the Duchess surprised style watchers by wearing one of the edgier labels on the London Fashion Week schedule, Le Kilt. Kate couldn't have looked less like a typical Le Kilt model when she arrived at St Catherine's Primary School teaming a Le Kilt design with a polo neck and heels. But in her own way, she not only paid a visual tribute to Scotland's famous garment, but also boosted a label seeking to modernize this traditional piece.

**LEFT** In Le Kilt on a trip to Edinburgh in February 2016.

# IN 'TENNIS BALL YELLOW' AT WIMBLEDON, 2016

Tennis has long been a passion for the Duchess of Cambridge, who is said to be a fierce opponent on the court. Even before her marriage to William, Kate was a regular in the Royal Box on Wimbledon's Centre Court, taking over as Royal Patron of the All England Lawn Tennis and Croquet Club from the Queen in 2017.

Over the years, Kate has delighted spectators with her Wimbledon looks. White is a favourite – 2011's tiered Temperley dress could have passed for a tennis skirt – and 2019's Dolce & Gabbana's lawn green frock was a clever allusion to the grass courts.

But it's 2016's 'tennis ball' dress that stands out as a literal dressing ace. The Duchess had worn the shift by London-based Serbian designer Roksanda, renowned for her brave, offbeat use of colour, during a tour to Australia. 'William said I look like a banana,' she revealed at the time. In the context of the tennis championship, though, it took on connotations of an unexpected but brilliantly appropriate object.

**LEFT** Kate wears Roksanda to Wimbledon, July 2016.

# IN JENNY PACKHAM TO LAUNCH NURSING NOW, 2018

Kate's visit to the Royal College of Obstetricians and Gynaecologists to launch a new campaign, Nursing Now, resulted in one of the Duchess's most heartfelt acts of literal dressing. Jenny Packham created an Empire-line royal blue silk dress with a matching tailored coat with white piped edging and buttons that skimmed over Kate's seven-month bump (she was expecting Prince Louis at the time).

The outfit mirrored the traditional colours associated with nurse's uniforms, which was underscored when Kate was pictured with Professor Lesley Regan, the college's then president, whose robes had very similar blue and white details.

'This campaign means a lot to me personally. My great-grandmother and grandmother were both volunteer nurses,' the Duchess said as she launched the Nursing Now campaign later that day. 'They would have learned first-hand from working with the Voluntary Aid Detachment and the Red Cross about the care and compassion that sometimes only nurses can provide.'

By dressing more like a nurse than a princess, the Duchess emphasized her admiration in the most captivating way imaginable.

# IN ERDEM FLORALS AT THE CHELSEA FLOWER SHOW, 2019

The Royal Horticultural Society's Chelsea Flower Show has a long association with the Royal Family; it is an annual tradition that the Queen is given a tour of the show, often accompanied by members of her family. Kate's first visit to the flower show came in 2016, when she wore a grass green dress coat by Catherine Walker & Co. The following year, she segued into even more literal territory in a botanical print dress by Rochas.

Many of the Royal Family have become involved in a more active way, too, and in 2019, the Duchess of Cambridge co-designed a 'Back to Nature' garden as part of her mission to get children playing and learning outside. Having taken a hands-on approach for several days before her garden's grand unveiling – wearing walking boots and outdoor jackets for the task – the Duchess arrived to show her creation to the Queen (who had contributed her own childhood memories of planting vegetables to inspire her granddaughter-in-law's design) wearing a Victorian-inspired dress decorated with a painterly floral print by Erdem (see page 61). The Duchess finished the look with Cassandra Goad pearl earrings and a pair of Castañer espadrille wedges, which became her go-to shoes that summer.

OPPOSITE The Duchess of Cambridge wears Jenny Packham for a visit to the Royal College of Obstetricians and Gynaecologists, London, February 2018.

## BEULAH ON WORLD ANTI-SLAVERY DAY, 2019

Beulah has been a favourite for the Duchess of Cambridge over the past decade. Established by her friends Lavinia Brennan and Lady Natasha Rufus Isaacs (who is married to one of Kate's old boyfriends, Rupert Finch), the label was founded to help the victims of trafficking.

On World Anti-Slavery Day in 2019, the Duchess was on the final day of her tour to Pakistan. While it might have appeared rather un-regal to sport the 'For Freedom' t-shirt that Beulah had created to mark the day, she opted for the label's Papilio coat as she visited the Army Canine Centre in Islamabad as a more subtle show of support.

'She is a wonderful ambassador for British clothes,' says Rufus Isaacs of the Duchess, 'and has helped tell and propel our story and mission to many people on an international scale.'

## EPONINE FOR A SPECIAL PERFORMANCE OF DEAR EVAN HANSEN, 2020

Sometimes, the Duchess's fashion choices seem so aptly imbued with messages that it is perhaps mere coincidence. However, given all we know about the meticulous planning that is involved in each engagement, it seems unlikely that such 'coincidences' are unplanned.

Kate has worn several outfits by the London-based label Eponine, which specializes in the 'elegant and classic shapes of the 1950s, '60s and '70s,' according to its founder Jet Shenkman.

When not designing, Jet is a psychotherapist and counsellor who has worked in bereavement support and set up low-cost services to help those who need it most. This passion must appeal to Kate, who has spearheaded campaigns to encourage more discussion of mental health.

So it seemed fitting that she chose a black tweed dress with crystal buttons by Eponine for a charity performance of *Dear Evan Hansen*, a musical that tackles the topic of mental health. 'If the Duchess wore the dress for that reason, I would be incredibly touched,' says Shenkman. 'I am so grateful for the way both the Duke and Duchess support mental health-related charities.'

**OPPOSITE** On a visit to the Army Canine Centre in Islamabad in October 2019, Kate chose a jacket from Beulah London.

**BELOW** Wearing Eponine, Kate arrives at the Noël Coward Theatre in London for a charity performance of *Dear Evan Hansen*, February 2020.

**RIGHT** Kate appears on ITV's *This Morning* wearing a dress by British brand Raey, May 2020.

THE DUCHESS OF CAMBRIDGE ON HER NEW PROJECT
#ThisMorning

# DRESSING FOR A CRISIS, 2020

When the Coronavirus crisis hit the UK in March 2020, Kate and William rapidly adapted, pivoting to video chats from their home Anmer Hall in Norfolk.

Can fashion be deployed when only your shoulders are in view? The Duchess proved it could. She adopted bright colours and graphic patterns that looked striking on screen, always being sensitive to source them from the high street, independent British labels or her own wardrobe. In a chat with veterans to mark VE Day, she chose a five-year-old dress by L.K. Bennett in a patriotic shade of vermillion, while a zigzag sweater by Tabitha Webb was debuted for a video call with midwives. When the Duchess appeared on television to launch the Hold Still initiative, she wore a lemon dress by Raey with an optimistic blossoming tree print; an acknowledgment in fashion form of the Royal Family's morale-boosting role.

The Duchess's style choices were not just visual messages. When the Cambridges appeared on the BBC's *The Big Night In* fundraising evening doing their 'Clap for Carers', they were all dressed in shades of blue. Kate's floral tea dress by British brand Ghost sold out and the brand announced that it would donate the proceeds to the NHS.

The birthday portraits that the Duchess shot of Prince Louis creating rainbow-painted handprints revealed how this symbol of hope struck a chord with Kate. She continued the theme in her own dressing, sticking to a spectrum of red, orange, yellow, green, blue, indigo and violet in her outfits.

# the STYLISTS

On 23 July 2013, the world was eagerly anticipating its first glimpse of the new royal baby. But an adjacent game of intrigue had begun after the Duchess of Cambridge's 'glam squad' were photographed arriving at the Lindo Wing. For style watchers, this was a moment almost as significant as Prince George's arrival, because Kate's stylist secret weapon was finally revealed.

Natasha Archer had worked for the Royal Household since 2007. Dressed in a low-key red floral tea dress and flat ballet pumps, her presence at the hospital, one of a small handful of non-family members to visit, was evidence of how important she had become to the Duchess. Not only had she been entrusted to deliver the pale blue spotted Jenny Packham dress that Kate would wear for one of the most significant photo opportunities of her royal life, but she had also reportedly had a hand in its creation.

Although she has never officially been called a stylist, Archer would go on to be credited for honing a regal look for Kate, researching possible designers for her to wear, liaising with brands to call in pieces and ensuring that for every public appearance the Duchess looked immaculate.

Though Archer's identity was known after those 2013 photographs, it would take a few more years for her true impact to become apparent.

Tales began to emerge of her commissioning bespoke items for the Duchess and finding ways to make looks suitable for royal engagements. In 2014, Kate's more polished, grown-up outfits during a tour to New Zealand and Australia were put down to Archer's influence, and in 2016, Indian designer Anita Dongre revealed that Archer had customized one of her dresses for Kate to wear during her visit to the country.

It was in Sydney during the 2014 tour that Kate and Natasha were photographed together for the first time, watching a rugby game. Both wearing grey sweaters, it was an image that revealed their friendship as well as their similar taste in clothes. In 2015, Archer was pictured at the same polo match as the Duchess and Prince George with both women wearing skinny jeans, and for a hike to the Tiger's Nest monastery in Bhutan in 2016, Natasha – as well as hairdresser Amanda Cook Tucker – joined the royal party.

Proof of Archer's role in organizing the Duchess's wardrobe has also come in snatched shots of her at airports on royal visits. She has been pictured everywhere from Canada to India, carrying garment bags embossed with the Duchess's initials and leather vanity cases or coordinating holdalls and suitcases, often alongside Cook Tucker or the Cambridge children's nanny, Maria Borrallo.

Like the Duchess, Natasha favours feminine tea and shift dresses, wedge sandals and sleek suede heels. When she married Getty's royal photographer Chris Jackson in 2017, Archer asked Jenny Packham – one of the Duchess's favourite designers – to create her wedding dresses, both of which incorporated nods to Kate's own bridal looks; the daytime gown had elegant lace sleeves and the evening creation came with a crystal belt and full skirt, just like the Duchess's own McQueen look.

In the 2019 New Year's Honours, Natasha was made a Member of the Royal Victorian Order – an honour that recognizes loyal service to the Royal Family. For the ceremony in which Prince William presented Archer with her order, she picked a navy and white spotted L.K. Bennett dress, accessorizing it with one of the Boleyn-style hatbands that had latterly become synonymous with the Duchess.

It was around this time that Kate chose to call in additional help with her style direction. While Archer was on maternity leave, the Duchess enlisted the assistance of Virginia Chadwyck-Healey, an old friend from St Andrews University who had gone on to become a retail editor at *Vogue.* Having just launched her own styling consultancy, Chadwyck-Healey was perfectly placed to help Kate add fashion nous to her wardrobe.

The way that Archer and Chadwyck-Healey work together has been a topic of debate. Although Archer is still instrumental in the everyday management of Kate's clothing, Chadwyck-Healey has helped shake things up, suggesting subtle upgrades that have made a big difference, from fresh labels and accessories to thinking of ways to revitalize older pieces.

Onita Prasada, owner of the O'nitaa boutique in Chelsea that Archer used to source many of the looks for the Pakistan tour, sums up Archer's contribution. 'Hats off to Natasha – the care she puts into everything is amazing,' she explains. 'When they were in Pakistan, William was about to walk out [in the outfit we had sourced for him]. She messaged me and said "Onita, I need help! What's the outfit called? I've left my phone in the UK." She's very good at what she does.'

Together, Archer and Chadwyck-Healy have become the Duchess of Cambridge's key style strategists, helping her create a signature look that has evolved over the past decade to be modern yet regal, youthful yet appropriate, and always imbued with thoughtful messages.

**RIGHT** Virginia Chadwyck-Healey at Royal Ascot, Berkshire in June 2019.

# KATE'S royal year

For anyone bemused by the enduring appeal of the Royal Family – an unelected entity that enjoys immense privilege and adoration by accident of birth – then perhaps the best explanation is its ability to provide a sense of continuity, stability and – often – wonder in an ever-changing world.

The Royal Family is, for many, like an anchor, and though realistically we know little about them aside from the brushstroke details they choose to share with us, they can feel like our own family too – we celebrate when they have a child or get married, we congratulate them on their birthday and they form part of our Christmas Day routine.

There is no better proof of the dependability of the Royal Family than a glance at its calendar, punctuated with occasions when we know they will come together and provide a stunning spectacle. During her first decade as a royal, the Duchess of Cambridge has found her place in these annual rituals, evolving from newcomer to confident supporting actor. It's a trajectory that will one day take her to Queen Consort.

Some themes have emerged in Kate's approach to dressing for these moments. Tailoring has emerged as an important ally for looking polished. In terms of colour palette, the Duchess displays a tacit understanding that she is not intended to be the focus at these events by choosing soft neutrals or pastels that photograph nicely without visually dominating. These are not times to trial new labels; instead she leans on a coterie of trusted designers to deliver immaculate, dependable pieces.

The royal year is a prism for studying the regal uniform that the Duchess has established, learning sartorial lessons from the Queen's creation of a timeless image that has become iconic.

This progress plays out in the Duchess's style choices for key occasions. At first she was finding her footing, establishing what Catherine, the Duchess might look like, rather than Kate, the royal girlfriend. There's a vast difference between dressing so as not to excite the paparazzi too much and navigating a way to look the part in photos that will be beamed around the world and be used again and again to tell the story of the late second Elizabethan age.

# MARCH, COMMONWEALTH DAY

On the second Monday in March, the Royal Family attends a service at Westminster Abbey to celebrate the Commonwealth. It was only in 2016, when the Duke and Duchess of Cambridge were edging into life as full-time royals, that they began to accompany the Queen to the event.

The Duchess made a fashion-forward impact at her first Commonwealth Day Service, wearing a grey coat with lace overlay by Canadian-born, London-based designer Erdem, which she paired with a wide-brimmed hat by Scottish milliner John Boyd – a clever combination drawing on talents from Commonwealth countries.

In 2020, there was seemingly a more personal slant to Kate's outfit. The service was the last royal engagement for the Duke and Duchess of Sussex as they stepped down as senior royals. After an emotional and fraught few months negotiating Meghan and Harry's departure, it was an important moment for the Royal Family to come together one final time.

Kate chose to wear the same red Catherine Walker & Co velvet-trimmed riding coat that she had first worn on Christmas Day in 2018, one of the handful of times that she was photographed chatting happily with Meghan in public. It served to recall seemingly happier times. The look was given a fresh flourish courtesy of a saucer hat by British milliner Sally-Ann Provan (see page 6).

**LEFT** Kate in Erdem at the Commonwealth Day Service at Westminster Abbey in March 2016.

**OPPOSITE** At a Buckingham Palace Garden Party wearing Emilia Wickstead in 2013.

# MARCH, ST PATRICK'S DAY

One of the annual rituals that the Duke and Duchess of Cambridge have made their own is the presentation of shamrock to the Irish Guards on St Patrick's Day. The Queen gave Prince William the honorary role of Royal Colonel of the Irish Guards in 2011.

Almost every year since then, the royal couple has visited the regiment for this ceremony. The day offers excellent photo opportunities, from the appearance of Domhnall, the regiment's Irish Wolfhound mascot, who is given his own sprig of shamrock by the Duchess, to the pint of Guinness or dram of whiskey that the couple share with soldiers after the formal proceedings.

As you might expect, Emerald Isle green is the Duchess's go-to hue for these engagements – a shade she deviated from only once in 2015, when she wore a chocolate brown coat by Catherine Walker & Co that complemented the khaki uniforms of the troops.

Most often, Kate has entrusted her St Patrick's Day looks to Alexander McQueen, Emilia Wickstead and Catherine Walker & Co, but she made an exception in 2014, when she opted for the £279 Persephone coat from British high-street store Hobbs. With its epaulettes, storm flaps and precise cut, the piece nods to the military theme of the day (see page 77).

# THE SUMMER GARDEN PARTIES

Over the course of every summer, the Queen invites 30,000 people to Garden Parties at Buckingham Palace and is joined by several senior members of her family at every gathering.

Kate has become a Garden Party regular, often opting for pretty pastel shades and details. Attending a party in May 2013, the Duchess had the added dilemma of dressing for the occasion at seven months pregnant. She embraced the challenge, wearing a bright yellow trapeze coat by Emilia Wickstead, whose sweeping shapes are brilliantly suited to maternity dressing. There was also something very Queenly about the bright colour and boxy silhouette of the coat.

Kate gave it her own twist by wearing it with patent cream stilettos by Russell & Bromley, a staple style in her 'shoe-drobe' around this time.

Kate chose buttercup-yellow McQueen for the Cambridges' first appearance as a family of five in 2019.

# JUNE, TROOPING THE COLOUR

This is the grand military parade and glorious balcony appearance that takes place each June in celebration of the Queen's official birthday.

On the second Saturday of the month, the most senior members of the Royal Family ride on horseback or in open-top carriages from Buckingham Palace to Horse Guards Parade, where the magnificent ceremony featuring the British Army's Infantry regiments takes place. Afterwards, the royals return to the palace and gather on the balcony to watch a fly-past by the Royal Air Force.

In her first year dressing for an event with such strong military tones, the Duchess of Cambridge chose a white Alexander McQueen frock coat. It was her first balcony appearance since her wedding, so it was clever to continue that theme not only by wearing the same designer but choosing a piece in white with the same exaggerated peplum detail.

In one of only two deviations from McQueen, in 2012 the Duchess turned to Erdem for a silver grey embroidered shift with a cowl neckline, which took advantage of this event

being all about waist-up dressing (most photographs are taken while sitting in a carriage or standing on the balcony).

More daring was the skirt suit by McQueen Kate chose in 2014. Its inverted notch collar plus a gobstopper pearl brooch offer waist-up interest but more intriguing are the skulls woven into the jacket's jacquard fabric.

In 2016, the Queen was celebrating her 90th birthday, so Trooping the Colour was extra special. It was also the first time that Princess Charlotte joined the balcony gathering. Kate rose to the occasion by re-wearing a McQueen coat and adding a Philip Treacy saucer hat with a giant silk rose in blush pink, coordinating with Charlotte in a dress of the same hue.

The Cambridges appeared as a fivesome in 2019 and demonstrated their prowess in coordinated dressing. With the children in shades of blue and the Duchess in pale yellow, they picked out the gold and royal blue accents on Prince William's Irish Guards tunic meticulously.

**ABOVE RIGHT, CENTRE AND RIGHT** Kate wore Alexander McQueen in 2011, 2014 and 2016.

# JUNE, THE ORDER OF THE GARTER CEREMONY

The Most Noble Order of the Garter is the oldest and most senior order of chivalry, founded by King Edward III in 1348. On the Monday before Royal Ascot each year, the Queen, honorary Royal Family members of the order and the Knights gather in Windsor for a lunch, service and procession through the town.

Kate first attended in 2008, when Prince William was installed as the thousandth Royal Knight and has been there almost every year since 2011, except when she's just had, or is about to have, a baby.

**LEFT** Kate in a Christopher Kane pale blue coat dress and Lock & Co. hat alongside Sophie, Countess of Wessex in 2014.

**OPPOSITE** Wearing Catherine Walker & Co. with Queen Letizia of Spain in 2019.

Most often, the duchess has not chosen this as an event where she attempts to wow – there's no hope of competing with the magnificent gold-braided navy velvet cloaks and feathered caps worn by the Knights, after all. A case in point was 2014, when she looked refined in a recycled ice blue Christopher Kane coat dress with a matching Lockand Co. hat.

An exception was made, however, in 2019 when King Felipe of Spain and King Willem-Alexander of the Netherlands were joining the order. This meant that their wives – Queen Letizia and Queen Máxima – would also be in attendance, joining the Duchess on the sidelines. As royal style leaders in their own rights, this was Kate's time to energize her Garter Day look.

She turned to Catherine Walker & Co for a pretty white coat dress with striking black rickrack trim. Of course, it may have been mere coincidence, but Kate's black and white ensemble toned perfectly with Queen Letizia's 1940s-style spotted dress by Spanish label Cherubina.

**LEFT** Kate chose
a white lace Dolce
& Gabbana dress for
her first appearance
at Royal Ascot in
June 2016.

**OPPOSITE** In
Elie Saab at Royal
Ascot, June 2019.

# JUNE, ROYAL ASCOT

Royal Ascot is said to be one of our racing-mad Queen's favourite times of year. The racecourse, situated near to Windsor Castle, becomes the world's most flamboyant show of fabulous fashion, with the Royal Family and their guests joining in with the spectacle.

Leaning on her love of literal dressing, Kate looked to one of Royal Ascot's most famous outfits ever (albeit a fictional one) as her style inspiration for her debut appearance in 2016, wearing a white lace dress by Dolce & Gabbana with a pale straw hat by Jane Taylor.

The outfit was immediately compared with Audrey Hepburn as Eliza Doolittle in the 'Ascot Gavotte' scene of the musical film *My Fair Lady*, in which Eliza is festooned in white lace. Why does Eliza Doolittle make an excellent royal racing reference? Because Cecil Beaton, favoured photographer of the Queen Mother, was responsible for her costumes.

The Duchess repeated the Doolittle inspiration in white McQueen lace in 2017, but in 2019 she gave it an update by wearing a pale blue ensemble by Lebanese designer Elie Saab, a favourite couturier to Middle Eastern royalty.

It was a look that proved Kate was becoming more adventurous in her choices – note the fresh proportions of the ankle-length skirt and pussy-bow neckline, plus the dotted tulle netting. This exciting confection was topped off with a Philip Treacy hat.

# NOVEMBER, REMEMBRANCE

This sombre time of year, when the Royal Family are at the centre of a period of national reflection on the loss of life in conflict, isn't about fashion. But that doesn't mean that there isn't a specific art in dressing to honour the memory of the dead without appearing needlessly ostentatious.

On the Saturday evening before Remembrance Sunday (which falls on the closest Sunday to 11 November), the Festival of Remembrance takes place at the Royal Albert Hall. An LBD is an obvious option for the evening and it was arguably Kate's first time at the event in 2015 that was the most noteworthy. She turned to Dolce & Gabbana for her lace dress, a classic piece from the Italian designers.

At Sunday's commemorations at the Cenotaph, even more sartorial rigour is required. In her first years standing on the balcony of the Foreign and Commonwealth Office overlooking the ceremony, the Duchess stuck to plain black items already in her wardrobe, but recently she has opted for pieces with military flair; 2018's Alexander McQueen coat was particularly chic with its cream raised collar, silver buttons and scarlet epaulettes. The Duchess wears three 'normal' poppies, one to represent each of the armed forces. She completes her collection with the special codebreaker poppy brooch in tribute to her grandmother, Valerie Glassborow, who worked at Bletchley Park where the German Enigma code was decrypted.

# DECEMBER, CHRISTMAS

One of the most joyful moments in the Royal calendar is Christmas, when the family gathers at Sandringham to celebrate. There is a demanding schedule to dress for, from the black tie dinner on Christmas Eve (when the Queen's favourite cocktail, a Zaza, is served) to two church services on Christmas morning, followed by lunch and, of course, the Queen's Speech in the afternoon.

It is the second morning church service that offers a festive fashion show, as the family walks from Sandringham House to St Mary Magdalene church. For her first royal Christmas outing, the Duchess had evidently put extensive thought into her look.

She debuted a new aubergine coat, the designer of which has never been revealed. A royal spokesman said at the time, 'The Duchess is keen to use independent British dressmakers, whose skills and craftsmanship she admires.' An 'Unidentified Fashion Object' as it's been dubbed by royal watchers is a rarity, with most of the Duchess's outfits either announced by Kensington Palace or discovered by the clever community of Kate aficionados.

**OPPOSITE** Two Remembrance Day looks: black lace Dolce & Gabbana at the Festival of Remembrance in 2015 and watching the National Service of Remembrance at the Cenotaph in Alexander McQueen in 2018.

**RIGHT** Kate teams a Moloh coat with a Lock & Co. pillbox-style hat at Sandringham in 2014.

The Duchess's first royal Christmas look also comprised a pair of bespoke black heels commissioned from Spanish label Mascaró, though she has never worn them again, and a trilby-with-a-twist by Jane Corbett. It was, however, her £1,900 Kiki McDonough earrings that grabbed the headlines, with plenty of theories that they were a Christmas gift from William.

After this bold first royal Christmas, Kate had a few years of keeping her festive looks low-key. In 2014, she debuted a new tweed coat that appeared to have a mysterious provenance but was eventually identified as being an old design by Moloh, a classic English country label based in Gloucestershire (see page 87).

Finishing the look with a brown 1960s pillbox hat and a scarf by Really Wild Clothing (another traditional brand), this epitomized Kate's natural predilection for heritage labels. Though she would have been conscious that pictures would be seen around the world, this style underlined the Cambridges' desire to be understated and was 'normal' as possible during this period.

Perhaps it was the presence of Meghan Markle for the first time, but Kate took her festive style up a notch in 2017 when she decided to wear a tartan coat by fashion-forward label Miu Miu. The coat offered a pitch-perfect way to telegraph festive cheer in a more fun and youthful way, as did the addition of a Dr Zhivago-style alpaca hat.

By 2019, Christmas at Sandringham was Meghan and Harry-less. The Cambridges stepped in to provide a refreshed sense of excitement, bringing Prince George and Princess Charlotte to the service for the first time. Now, rather than dressing for herself or to match Meghan in the fashion stakes, it was her daughter whom Kate considered in her Christmas dressing approach.

**OPPOSITE** Kate wearing a Miu Miu coat to the Christmas Day church service in Sandringham in December 2017.

**RIGHT** Wearing a Lock & Co. hat and green suede Emmy London heels that perfectly coordinated with Princess Charlotte's coat in December 2019. Kate's coat is by Catherine Walker & Co.

That she debuted a bespoke new mohair coat by Catherine Walker & Co was proof of the Duchess's newly upscale Christmas style, showing her as a senior royal rather than just one of the family. She may have looked elegantly regal, but Kate admitted to a member of the public that she was too hot and 'really shouldn't have worn this'.

Even if Kate did have cause to regret the coat, she must have been pleased with the accessories; her recycled forest green Lock & Co. hat and Josie block heels from Emmy London coordinated beautifully with four-year-old Charlotte's double-breasted Amaia Kids coat – a masterclass in mother-daughter dressing.

# casual KATE

Until Kate came along, the only time you'd be likely to spot the royals in
relaxed attire was when they were photographed 'off duty' at horse shows
or polo matches. These snatched glimpses revealed something of their true,
sartorial preferences; the Queen's love of knotting a silk scarf was cemented
by her appearances at the Badminton Horse Trials as far back as the 1950s.

If Her Majesty has her headscarves, then Kate will forever be associated with her beloved skinny jeans. One of the style hallmarks of her early years as a royal, this is one piece that has remained consistent while other early favourites fell by the wayside.

It's not just in the very occasional insights we get into Kate in private that tell us that she loves skinny jeans. She's the first royal to turn dressing down into an art form, and is as likely to be seen in trainers or practical coats on engagements as she is in sophisticated couture. This is one area of royal dressing that Kate has been the first to adopt on such a scale, and it's been an essential tool in shaping her sporty, down-to-earth reputation; 'The Duchess is a keen sportswoman,' her official website emphasizes. The patronages she has chosen to take on reflect this. SportsAid, the 1851 Trust (which helps young people from all backgrounds to get into sailing) and the Lawn Tennis Association are among the charities closest to her heart, and when she visits them, she's as likely to be in sportswear that allows her to get involved as she is a new designer look.

Many of her fans confess to preferring Kate's casual outings over her more dazzling ensembles. It feels refreshing to see a future queen in pieces many of us wear in our everyday lives. Kate's royal casual dressing revolution is really down to what feels right for now. No one would have expected the Queen and Prince Philip to go head to head in a sailing competition 50 years ago, when the monarchy was still renowned for its stoic, ceremonial appearance and long before exercise had been promoted as a salve for both physical and mental health.

Kate and William have also had the luxury of beginning their royal life when the Duke is second in line to the throne, so there has been time to focus on causes and activities that appeal to them personally rather than having all their time consumed by state duties. With their shared love of sport and outdoor pursuits, it's only natural that the couple have geared their focus to these areas as they carve their own royal path.

When she visited her old school St Andrews in Berkshire in 2012, the Duchess said that 'It was while I was here at school that I realized my love of sport. Sport has been a huge part of my life, and I feel incredibly grateful for the opportunities I had to get outside and play in such wonderful open spaces.'

That day was one of the rare times that Kate dressed rather incongruously for the occasion; she had deftly chosen a tartan Alexander McQueen coat in honour of St Andrew (the patron saint of Scotland) and high-heeled boots, but didn't change to try out the school's new hockey pitch. 'Hockey in Heels' was a gift to headline writers.

# THE QUEEN OF SKINNY JEANS

There is no better codifier of 'everywoman' in the 21st century than skinny jeans. It was supermodel Kate Moss who first made them famous as a key component of her artfully thrown-together indie look in the early noughties. On the Venn diagram of Moss vs Middleton style, it's skinny jeans where the two women meet. But if Moss's styling was rock chic, then Middleton deployed her skinny jeans as a sleek way to do casual dressing.

Kate loved the look before getting married, often wearing jeans tucked into boots. But the Duchess's decision to make them a cornerstone of her royal wardrobe has been game changing, with skinny jeans making up part of her 'on duty' look for the first time during the tour to Canada in 2011. Through pregnancy and her gently evolving style over the years, skinnies sourced everywhere from Zara to J Brand have been a constant.

In 2012, Kate was at peak sporty mode thanks to her role as an ambassador for the London Olympics. Perhaps as a nod to the bright colours of the Games' logo, she chose this time to experiment with jeans in vivid shades of cobalt and coral. Taking part in a training session with the British hockey team, the Duchess added zing to her official hoodie and Adidas trainers with bright new Zara jeans. It was evidently a look that resonated; Asda saw a 471% rise in sales of a similar style.

**OPPOSITE** Kate in Zara jeans to play hockey on a visit to the Olympic Park in Stratford, London in March 2012.

# SNOWY SCOUTING

When the Duchess lived in Anglesey in the early years of her marriage, she volunteered as a Scout leader. With happy memories of being a Brownie as a child, the organization encapsulates her love of being outdoors. That love was put to the test in March 2013, when she visited a Scout camp in Cumbria in the midst of a blizzard. Unperturbed, the Duchess joined in with baking bread over the campfire and encouraging the children.

Kate's off- and on-duty casual wardrobes often cross over, as evidenced by her decision to wear wellies by French outdoor brand Le Chameau. This upmarket style is favoured by the countryside cognoscenti thanks to their cosy neoprene lining. Her outfit was completed with more classic country favourites: a Barbour jacket and cap from Really Wild Clothing. The final flourish, of course, was her red, white and blue Scout's neckerchief.

**LEFT** In a Barbour jacket and Le Chameau boots at Great Tower Scout camp, Cumbria, March 2013.

# THE POST-BIRTH COMEBACK

If Kate's casual outings are a way to appear relatable and normal, then this appearance, at a day of SportsAid workshops, three months after the birth of Prince George, did more to suggest the Duchess's superwoman status.

Her new mum essentials of stretchy jeans (by J Brand) and a striped top (by Ralph Lauren) were smartened up with a blazer by Smythe and astonishingly high cork wedges by Stuart Weitzman – although she did tell one of the organizers that she wished she'd brought trainers. A shot of Kate playing volleyball was a gift to newspapers, as she reached up to reveal a flat stomach. 'Ab fab!', 'No mummy tummy' and 'By George, she's fab' were just a few of the headlines that made it onto front pages the following day.

**LEFT** Kate wears J Brand jeans and a Smythe blazer at the SportsAid Athlete Workshop at the Olympic Park in Stratford, London in October 2013.

# Kate in Vogue

The Duchess of Cambridge has inevitably become a style icon, but her eagerness and determination not to become defined by fashion is no better exemplified than in the tale of her cover for British *Vogue*'s centenary issue in April 2016.

Kate was top of every magazine editor's wish list of cover stars after her engagement, but she turned down every request. No doubt she was anxious not to be seen to be leaning too heavily into the glitzy superstar potential of her new role and to avoid comparisons with Diana, Princess of Wales, who had posed for several glossy magazine covers in the 1990s.

But when *Vogue* teamed up with the National Portrait Gallery to put on the *Vogue 100: A Century of Style* exhibition to mark its 100th birthday, there was a compelling reason for the Duchess to consider the proposal. As patron of the gallery, the shoot could be positioned as her seeking to support an artistic cause to which she was devoted, rather than embracing the chance to be photographed in the latest fashions.

Everything about the shoot that eventually took place typifies Kate as a down-to-earth duchess, devoid of airs and graces, preferring fresh air and fields to being trussed up in haute couture. Not only was this Kate's comfort zone, but it was a million miles from the royal fashion shoots of previous generations.

'It was very clear from the outset that these pictures were to be of the woman herself rather than of a figurehead, and that they would be as informal as possible,' wrote Alexandra Shulman, *Vogue*'s then editor-in-chief, of the planning for the cover. 'The Duchess liked the idea of being photographed in the countryside, and she wanted the pictures to reflect an element of her private existence. She didn't want to be dressed as a fashion plate and was not keen to be shot in gala gowns and tiaras.'

Fashion-wise, this was Casual Kate as she had never been seen before. 'The clothes *Vogue*'s fashion director Lucinda Chambers gathered for the day were based on what the Duchess likes to wear when she is off duty – jeans, shirts, t-shirts. The same as the rest of us,' wrote Shulman.

But in reality, these were quite different to the pieces already in Kate's wardrobe. The Breton top, by French label Petit Bateau, is more structured and colourful than her usual favourites. Skinny jeans were eschewed in favour of more fashion-forward cuts; the shoot included 7 For All Mankind's '70s-style wide-legged palazzo jeans and AG Jeans' flared dungarees. On the cover, Kate wore a wide-lapelled suede trench coat and white shirt by Burberry – timeless designs, but not items she had been seen in before. The look was topped off with a vintage fedora.

Although Kate and William had previously been captured by Diana and *Vogue* favourite Mario Testino, the Duchess asked that a less-established name be given the opportunity to take her *Vogue* pictures. British photographer Josh Olins was eventually given the commission thanks to the 'quiet elegance of his work and his "woman", who has polish but also a degree of understatement,' according to Shulman. It's a description that would no doubt have appealed to Kate.

The Duchess seems to have embodied this low-fuss approach during the shoot. Olins remembered her coming to look through the clothes rail the day before with her children in tow, enjoying a cup of tea as she perused the options. The following morning, she arrived with her hair in rollers, and spent the day generally trying to make everything as relaxed as possible for the crew as they shot in the Norfolk fields near to Anmer Hall, the Cambridges' country home, on a biting cold January day.

'The process of the shoot was fascinating to see,' the Duchess later told *Vogue*. 'It was so much closer to the process of painting a portrait than I had appreciated before, seeing the layers of the setting, make-up, clothes and light all coming together to form the final image. Seeing everything come together at once made me realize how much work goes into a single image.'

**BELOW** Kate wears Alexander McQueen to visit the *Vogue 100: A Century of Style* exhibition at the National Portrait Gallery, London in May 2016.

The Duchess of Cambridge in
a Perfect Moment jacket at the
Queen Elizabeth Olympic Park,
London, in February 2017.

# SPORTS STYLE

The Duchess hasn't always depended on skinny jeans for sporty engagements. Sometimes she arrives in an elegant outfit before changing into something more suitable, as on this visit to Edinburgh where she swapped a Sportmax coat, black polo neck and kilt for an outfit she might wear for a game of tennis.

Taking part in a 'Tennis on the Road' workshop run by Judy Murray (mother to tennis champions Andy and Jamie), Kate championed sporting giants and under-the-radar workout labels alike.

Her tuxedo-style track pants – from Monreal London,

founded by pro tennis player Steffani Grosse – were a clever solution for a royal workout in front of the cameras, reading as simultaneously smart and sporty. Their £259 price tag was a reminder of Kate's generous clothing budget, but also shows her buying into one of the many luxe athleisure labels that have emerged in recent years. More attainable were the £40 Nike top and box-fresh Asics trainers that completed the outfit.

**RIGHT** The Duchess in Monreal London and Nike to play tennis in Edinburgh in February 2016.

# DOING THE PUFFER TREND

One of the Duchess's most famous 'action' shots was snapped in February 2017, in the run-up to the London Marathon. That year, the Heads Together campaign, spearheaded by Kate, William and Harry, partnered with the race in order to raise awareness and create what was described as a 'mental health marathon'.

The young royals joined a training session in East London that would later form part of a documentary about a group of runners' journeys to completing the 26.2-mile challenge. This was an apt showcase for the Cambridges' and Prince Harry's love of a fun, relaxed engagement.

Practicality was undoubtedly high on the Duchess's list of priorities, as most of the visit took place outside and a relay race was a highlight of the itinerary. While she didn't stray from her beloved skinny jeans, Kate did update her casual look with a neat-fitting bright red puffer jacket by upmarket ski label Perfect Moment.

Kate also debuted a pair of New Balance trainers, part of a collaboration with gymwear brand Sweaty Betty, which were put to the test when Kate completed a 50-metre sprint. The final, slightly less athletic touch? A £3,100 pair of Asprey diamond button earrings.

# A SHORTS FIRST

Why is an outfit put together entirely of kit sourced from Gill Marine, a sailing apparel supplier, of note in Kate's fashion evolution? Because this was the first time that she was photographed wearing shorts as a royal, while taking part in a regatta on the Isle of Wight in August 2019 (see page 90). An item that might be a no-brainer for casual summer dressing for most women, shorts are notable in a regal context because they're both sporty and revealing.

Although the Duchess has not chosen to be vocal about having feminist credentials in the same way as her sister-in-law Meghan, she does suggest that actions can speak louder than words. This was a royal milestone because it showed her dressing purely for the task at hand – a day of sailing to raise funds for charity as part of the King's Cup Regatta, an initiative started by King George V in 1920 and revived by Kate and William as a way to fundraise for their charities.

The Duchess's sailing kit message? Girls, get active – and don't worry about looking glamorous while you're at it.

**OPPOSITE** Kate wears a Philosophy di Lorenzo Serafini blazer and skinny jeans to a graduation ceremony for sports coaching apprentices at West Ham United football club's London Stadium in October 2017.

# THE SMART-CASUAL FORMULA

There's a big difference between sporty and glossy, and there have been plenty of moments when Kate has needed something 'in between', allowing her to exhibit sporting prowess while also delivering a sense of formality.

The Duchess has landed on a trusty formula for these visits, which goes something like this: tailored blazer + black polo neck + black skinny jeans + black heeled boots. The black canvas is streamlined and unfussy and therefore camera-friendly, while the blazer enlivens and elevates the look with a splash of colour.

An excellent example of this combination in action came in October 2017, when Kate accompanied William and Harry to a graduation ceremony for sports coaching apprentices. It was this outfit that cemented the Duchess's favoured new smart-casual go-to, as she wore a pale blue, double-breasted Philosophy di Lorenzo Serafini blazer – a style she also owns in red and had worn in the same way a few months earlier. With its shiny gold buttons, the jacket added a military feel. Along with faded black jeans and a turtleneck, Kate also wore heeled Chelsea boots by Russell & Bromley.

As she was in the early stages of her pregnancy with Prince Louis, and suffering from hyperemesis gravidarum once again, this was a tried-and-tested look to put together without too much effort. But it also confirmed this as a signature Kate outfit, one she has recreated several times since with different blazers. It's also an accessible look for her admirers to emulate – even if they can't stretch to a £750 jacket.

# A NEW CASUAL

Just in case we were in danger of assuming that Kate in casual mode must always include skinny jeans, for the Chelsea Flower Show in 2019, the Duchess upgraded her dress-down repertoire.

For a morning showing children the 'Back to Nature' garden she had co-designed, Kate wore an outfit comprised of high-waisted linen culottes and a broderie anglaise blouse by M.i.h Jeans. It was fitting that the cropped trousers came from Massimo Dutti, big sister of Zara, Kate's favourite source of skinny jeans – she'd chosen the grown-up brand for a more grown-up look.

That she chose this engagement to wear an outfit that was such a departure from her casual norm was no coincidence. The Chelsea Garden Show project had been praised by royal commentators as an example of Kate growing in confidence. The change in her clothes was a visual signal of how far she'd come.

**RIGHT** The Duchess of Cambridge on a visit to the RHS Chelsea Flower Show in May 2019.

## Casual favourite: Troy

If the Duchess's formal wardrobe is very much a reflection of her royal role, then her more casual choices provide an insight into how Kate – a normal, countryside-loving, 30-something mum – might dress if she weren't an HRH.

One way she's done this is to wear pieces from brands started by her friends, whose ethos reflects her own personal style and lifestyle. Troy London was founded in 2014 by sisters Lucia Ruck Keene and Rosie Van Cutsem, who is one of the Cambridges' Norfolk neighbours and married to William Van Cutsem, Prince George's godfather. Their brand has reimagined country favourites like wax jackets and gilets with a modern twist.

'Our designs are inspired by heritage British "country style" and designed to suit the busy modern woman,' says Van Cutsem. 'Our jackets, coats and wardrobe staples all have a distinctly British flair and are stylish, but also work on a technical level. We love to celebrate the beautiful styles, fabrics and craftsmanship available in this country and hope to ensure the special details and contemporary styling make for pieces that will feel unique and special, season after season.'

Kate has three Troy jackets that she's been wearing since 2016, a show of support that has undoubtedly helped to raise the label's profile. Visiting the Lake District in June 2019, the Duchess was in her beloved skinny jeans but smartened the look with some significant new pieces – Troy's £275 cotton Tracker jacket, which Van Cutsem describes as having 'a soft colour palette and an elegant silhouette'.

The jacket was teamed with more on-trend additions; a pretty pie-crust collar blouse by French label Sézane alludes to a style that

**ABOVE** The Duke and Duchess of Cambridge meet members of the public as they visit the Market Square in Keswick on a trip to Cumbria in June 2019.

Princess Diana loved to wear in the early 1980s and which has been having a fashion moment again in the past few years. Kate's final style-conscious swap was a pair of chunky See By Chloé hiking boots, arguably more practical and fashionable than the wedges or heels she might have chosen earlier in her marriage.

# MOTHERHOOD

The royal family depends upon continuity, and continuity only comes with babies. Once those babies arrive, several years of public cheer – and excellent PR – are practically guaranteed, as the new royal generation charms the world.

'People are bound to ask...children, do you want lots of children?' asked Tom Bradby when he interviewed the couple to mark their engagement. 'I think we'll take it one step at a time,' William replied. 'We'll sort of get over the marriage first and then maybe look at the kids. But obviously we want a family, so we'll have to start thinking about that.' Any other answer would have been distinctly un-royal.

Kate and William resisted the tradition of starting their family immediately – Prince Charles was born six days short of his parents' first wedding anniversary and Prince William arrived 11 months after Charles and Diana's marriage. The year 2012 was a historic one in the UK, with the London Olympics and the Queen's Diamond Jubilee, so the Duke and Duchess took their time settling into married life as well as undertaking a tour to South East Asia and the South Pacific to mark Her Majesty's 60th year on the throne.

That the Cambridges announced that they were expecting their first child at the start of December that year could be interpreted as a brilliantly timed cherry on the cake. The country – and world – was hopeful of a cause for celebration in the summer of 2013.

By 2018, the Duke and Duchess had more than done their duty, providing an heir, a spare and a spare spare. What's more, they had expanded their distinctive Cambridge brand. What began as a fairytale story of a normal girl marrying a prince had become a quintessential, idealized British family.

Everything from Kate and William's children's names to the clothing they dress them in has evoked fascination and debate, but the strategy is best described as traditional with a modern, relatable gloss; George, Charlotte and Louis may be monikers that pay tribute to previous kings, queens and royal mentors, but they fit in with any other child in a Norfolk or Kensington playground, and for every smocked romper suit or Liberty print dress, a Cambridge child will have a John Lewis cardigan or scuffed pair of plimsolls.

The Duchess has been a key architect of this approach. Though the Cambridges have sought to keep their family life private, they recognize that the world wishes to see their children grow up and have orchestrated occasional public appearances to offer a small insight into their childhoods. In these moments, we not only see the children but Kate as a mother – rather than Duchess, charity patron or future queen – too.

On tours and the few official engagements that the children have carried out, we witness Kate juggling her roles in looks that must consider even more complex factors than usual. At other times, we are afforded a glimpse into what normal – or a polished version thereof – looks like for the Cambridge clan, whether that's in snapshots of life at their country home, Anmer Hall in Norfolk, or outings to watch William play in polo matches.

As in every other aspect of her wardrobe, the Duchess puts careful thought into what her style choices tell us about who she is as a mother and what her family represents.

# THE LINDO WING

Some of the most famous images of Kate have been taken in the inauspicious location that is the steps leading up to the private Lindo Wing of St Mary's Hospital in Paddington where the Duchess has given birth to her three children.

In the weeks leading up to her deliveries, this area has been overtaken by royal baby mania, with photographers staking their pitches and waiting in frenzied anticipation for a glimpse of the latest royal arrival.

Problematic though it might seem to expect a woman who has been through labour just hours earlier to face the glare of the media, the Duchess has always seemed to take these moments in good spirits, trading post-birth bliss for a blow-dry, a full face of make-up and heels in order to prepare for a few minutes in front of the cameras.

In an interview with Giovanna Fletcher on her *Happy Mum, Happy Baby* podcast in 2020, Kate spoke about the mixed emotions of these photocalls. 'Slightly terrifying, slightly terrifying, I'm not going to lie,' she confided. But she added, 'Everyone had been so supportive and both William and I were really conscious that this was something that everyone was excited about, and you know we're hugely grateful for the support that the public had shown us, and actually for us to be able to share that joy and appreciation with the public I felt was really important.'

So, what to wear? For every Lindo Wing appearance, Kate's approach has been tweaked, sending a slightly different message about the balance of motherhood and majesty.

You might assume that the introduction of Prince George would have been the most formal occasion. After all, this was not only Kate and William's newborn son but a future king. Yet the Duchess looked remarkably carefree when she stepped out of the hospital the day after the arrival, debuting a floaty blue and white polka dot dress by Jenny Packham that she wore with old favourite Pied A Terre espadrille wedges and a straight, low-key blow-dry. It is thought that a pink version of the dress existed in case the baby had been a girl.

Despite appearing effortlessly simple, the look was laden with subtle meaning and emotion. Kate exuded new mother radiance, yet by choosing the

**OPPOSITE** Prince Charles and Princess Diana leaving the Lindo Wing after the birth of their first son, Prince William, in 1982.

**RIGHT** William and Kate on the same steps as they leave the Lindo Wing with newborn son Prince George in July 2013.

same pattern worn by Princess Diana to introduce William on the same hospital steps 31 years before, the grandmother baby George would never meet became part of the moment and the continuity of the monarchy was emphasized to the world.

For Princess Charlotte's debut two years later, in May 2015, the effect was decidedly more 'superwoman'; a sign that Kate interpreted this moment as part of her duty as a future queen and princess.

Emerging within hours of her daughter's birth, the sight of the Duchess in a mostly white shift dress made mothers the world over simultaneously wince and gasp in admiration. The Jenny Packham dress was decorated with a delicate pale yellow buttercup print, but the rest of the ensemble did little to acknowledge the Duchess's recent labour; she was wearing 3¼-inch Jimmy Choo cream heels, while her bouncy, curled hair and 'done' make-up this time were more suggestive of an official engagement than a hospital departure.

**LEFT** The Duke and Duchess of Cambridge emerge from the Lindo Wing with baby Charlotte in 2015. Again, Kate wore Jenny Packham.

In a remarkable coincidence of patriotism and nature, the Cambridges' third child was born on St George's Day 2018 and – somehow – the Duchess had the outfit to match. Jenny Packham had once again made the dress, and this time they chose a red and white design. Not only did this echo England's St George's Cross flag, but they were also the colours worn by Princess Diana leaving hospital with Prince Harry in 1984. Accessorized with the Queen's pearl and diamond earrings, the Duchess had managed to weave both a national and personal story into her look.

**ABOVE** Princess Diana leaving the Lindo Wing after the birth of Prince Harry in 1984.

**RIGHT** Kate and William leaving St Mary's with Prince Louis in 2018. Kate is in Jenny Packham.

# ON TOUR

Royal children were once left at home in the care of nannies while their parents undertook international tours. Now, where appropriate, they come along, too – and become the stars of the show. Fashion-wise, this means that the wardrobe considerations are not limited only to what the Duchess chooses to wear, but how it will coordinate in family pictures.

The first test of this balancing act came during 2014's tour to New Zealand when Prince George was just eight months old. One of the first engagements of the trip was a playdate with New Zealand babies hosted by Plunket, an organization that provides support and well-being services for the country's under-fives. Kate and her son pulled off a matching look; the Duchess chose a wave-patterned dress by US designer Tory Burch that reflected the smocking on George's boat-embroidered dungarees by British childrenswear designer Rachel Riley. The nautical element tied their outfits together, while the black and white pattern of the Duchess's dress was a nod to an important colour combination in New Zealand culture.

By the time of 2016's tour to Canada, Princess Charlotte had arrived. The Cambridges made an appearance as a foursome at a children's tea party at Government House in Victoria. With William, George and Charlotte in shades of blue and red, reflecting the British Columbia flag, the Duchess opted for a dress that was playfully appropriate and regally brave; few mothers would dare wear cream while supervising their children, especially in front of the world's media, but Kate's See By Chloé dress remained immaculate throughout (see page 104). One concession to practicality was the decision to wear wedges (from high-street label Monsoon) rather than heels.

The following year, in Germany, the Cambridges cut a dash on the tarmac in a synchronized demonstration of diplomatic dressing. Though the Duchess usually loves to channel a country's flag, the red, orange and black hues of the German flag are perhaps a little tricky to translate elegantly. Instead, the family were all dressed in variations of cornflower blue, a bright yet soft shade in homage to the country's national flower. The arrival in Germany was the first time that the Princess, only two years old, had accepted her own posy and given a curtsy in thanks. She was also already demonstrating a mastery of dressing diplomatically.

**LEFT** Kate in a Tory Burch dress at an event for Plunket nurses and parents at Government House, Wellington, New Zealand, 2014.

Kate in Catherine Walker & Co arriving at Berlin Airport with William, George and Charlotte for a visit to Germany, July 2017.

Kate in a Me+Em reverse-stripe Breton top and skinny jeans at the Beaufort Polo Club, 2015.

# AT THE POLO

If Kate and William have been keen to shield their children from public view, then one of the few concessions they have made – aside from a handful of tours and Trooping the Colour sightings – is the polo. Each summer, the Prince plays several charity matches and often Kate and the children come along to watch. In this setting, photographers can capture the family enjoying a summer day out with little intrusion.

At the polo, the Duchess is in mum mode. Yes, she's aware that she'll be photographed, but the focus is on looks that are practical, so here we see her switch up some of her usual 'royal uniform' tropes, while other aspects are familiar, cementing them as Kate signatures.

Many mothers will relate to the look that the Duchess chose in one of her earlier polo outings with a toddler Prince George at the Beaufort Polo Club in 2015: skinny jeans from Topshop, a Breton top from Me+Em, a pair of Sebago boat shoes (which she's worn numerous times, both on and off duty) and Ray-Ban Wayfarer sunglasses. It's a classic weekend ensemble that semaphores casual normality – that the Duchess has never tried to make a fashion parade of the polo has been a key part of building the relatable, down-to-earth aspect of the Cambridge brand.

She did opt for something slightly more upscale, though still accessible, for another polo match in June 2018. That day she was photographed wearing a striped cotton design from the Spanish retailer Zara, and the previous month she'd taken George and Charlotte to the Houghton Horse Trials sporting a similar blue cotton Zara dress with black embroidery.

The Duchess elevated her polo look with her white Victoria Beckham handbag, a roomy tote that she'd previously carried at Wimbledon. In the context of a day out with the children, it was a practical accessory and there were snaps of George and Charlotte rummaging inside for toys and snacks.

If Kate had demonstrated her penchant for a high-street style refresh, then in 2019 she used her polo outing to remind us of her willingness to delve

into her wardrobe for something appropriate. By the time she debuted her L.K. Bennett Madison tea dress in a public setting, the silk design was long since sold out – she'd already worn it in a different colour in 2015. The Duchess paired the look with the Castañer wedges that she wore five times that summer and Ray-Bans.

But her most notable accessory upgrade for an afternoon running around after three children was a new Mulberry bag worn cross-body, keeping Kate's hands free for scooping up Louis and handing out drinks. It's a contrast to the usual function of a bag for the Duchess – to keep her hands occupied while on official duty.

**RIGHT** Kate in a Zara midi dress at the Maserati Royal Charity Polo Trophy in 2018.

## ON THE SCHOOL RUN

When William and Harry attended Wetherby School as children, Princess Diana's school-run style became a subject of fascination with the press. Now there is an agreement that Kate and William can drop off their children at Thomas's Battersea in peace, but dressing for the school gates is a yummy mummy phenomenon – some opt for pilates-ready ensembles, while others are dressed for work. The Duchess most likely zigzags between these extremes, depending on her schedule.

In exchange for privacy the rest of the time, the Cambridges allowed cameras to capture Prince George and Princess Charlotte's first days of school. William accompanied George alone in 2017, as Kate was suffering from severe morning sickness, but in 2019 we had a glimpse of her school-run look, albeit a camera-ready version.

The Duchess echoed the blue and red shades of her children's uniforms in a floral Michael Kors midi. The look incorporated classic Cambridge relatability; the dress was one that Kate had previously worn and she was radiant thanks to a summer tan. But a glossy blow-dry, Prada heels and a pair of Asprey diamond earrings all served as reminders that this was a very royal first day at school.

## PIPPA'S WEDDING

The Duchess has attended dozens of weddings over the years, but none so personal as that of her sister Pippa Middleton in the summer of 2017. And if confirmation were required that this was a special moment for Kate, then we need only look to the outfit the Duchess commissioned for the day, on which she acted as a supervisor to the adorable gaggle of bridesmaids and pageboys, among them Prince George and Princess Charlotte.

For previous weddings, the Duchess has tended to take two routes, either re-wearing an old outfit so as not to upstage the bride, or, for high-profile nuptials like Harry and Meghan's or Princess Eugenie and Jack Brooksbank's weddings, she has turned to Alexander McQueen for something tailored and formal.

Although McQueen was once again the chosen designer for Pippa's marriage to James Matthews, Kate adjusted her look to be softer and more romantic. Not only was this in keeping with the bucolic village setting, but it also exemplified her as a sister and mother. Arguably, the look was one of her loveliest; the dusky rose silk dress came with delicately billowing balloon sleeves and was completed by a Jane Taylor rose-adorned hat. Another indication of the day's importance to Kate was a new pair of Kiki McDonough diamond and morganite earrings to match the dress.

The Duchess had played an informal but crucial part in the day, sketching the church for the order of service, keeping the bridal party in order and reading a prayer during the service. So although she was dressed more like a guest than a matron of honour, it was entirely fitting that Kate's outfit matched the sashes on the bridesmaids' dresses, which were bespoke designs by Pepa & Co., one of Kate's favoured childrenswear labels. This attention to detail made for picture-perfect scenes as the Duchess revelled in her role.

**OPPOSITE** For Princess Charlotte's first day at school in September 2019, Kate chose a Michael Kors midi dress.

**BELOW** In Alexander McQueen for sister Pippa's wedding to James Matthews, May 2017.

OPPOSITE Kate wears Alexander McQueen at the 73rd British Academy Film Awards at the Royal Albert Hall, February 2020.

# REGAL glamour

'I'm really sorry I'm not wearing a pretty dress today,' the Duchess of Cambridge told a Cinderella-mad little girl she met on a visit to Wales in February 2020. That day, Kate was wearing a navy Hobbs coat layered over a Zara sweater dress. Hardly the stuff of Princess fairytales.

But had that little girl seen the Duchess just two days earlier, she would almost certainly have been thrilled by her princess-like appearance. At the British Academy Film Awards, or BAFTAs, that night, the Duchess glittered in a gold-embroidered McQueen gown offset by Van Cleef & Arpels jewels and sparkling Jimmy Choo heels.

For most women, this is a once-in-a-blue-moon look, but for a duchess it is all in a day's work. Kate and William have revolutionized royal public relations by emphasizing their normality, but they have juggled that with an understanding that sometimes only glitz and glamour will do. The royal job is about attending events where they are the star attraction, so it would be disappointing if the Duchess chose these moments to be 'relatable'. This is her chance to shine and to fully embrace her royal status.

Royal fashion website UFO No More has been adding up royal fashion expenditure since 2017, establishing that Kate spent around £115,000 in 2017, £70,000 in 2018 and £60,000 in 2019. These might seem like huge amounts, but they don't include bespoke pieces, the prices of which aren't documented but would be thousands of pounds each and that are often worn for these galas, receptions, premieres and dinners.

The Duchess's wardrobe is funded privately, through William's own fortune and money the couple receive from Prince Charles' Duchy of Cornwall income. She cannot accept clothing for free, so there are significant costs attached to the business of being a stylish young royal. But Kate has also been careful to balance ostentation with the impression of occasional thrift, throwing in a recycled gown or off-the-rack frock. In doing so, she has managed to avoid criticism that she might be spending too much on clothes. As a future queen, an arsenal of eveningwear is essential in crafting an image of modern regal magic.

# A DAZZLING START

In 2011, courtiers were careful not to have Kate doing too much too soon, as had happened with Diana. And yet the public desire for any glimpse of William's new wife was unquenchable, and a chance for guaranteed positive press and renewed enthusiasm must have been irresistible after more than a decade of lacklustre coverage for the Windsors.

The new Duchess was mostly known as a middle-class, sporty girl, and while a handful of post-engagement public appearances and the spectacular wedding certainly shifted that mindset, a few displays of regal razzle-dazzle wouldn't go amiss. So within three months of being married, the Duchess had enjoyed two fabulously successful red-carpet moments, which are still among her best remembered almost a decade on.

The first was only her third public appearance after the wedding festivities, a gala at Kensington Palace to celebrate the 10th anniversary of ARK (Absolute Return for Kids), a charity founded by a group of hedge financiers including Arpad Busson, former partner of Elle Macpherson and Uma Thurman.

Kate looked radiant in a sequinned gown by Jenny Packham, the first time she wore the designer who would go on to become a favourite. It's little wonder

**LEFT** The Duchess of Cambridge in Jenny Packham at the ARK (Absolute Return for Kids) 10th Anniversary Gala Dinner.

judging by the success of this first creation, which served to enhance Kate's fresh-from-honeymoon newlywed glow. With its fluttery tulle cap sleeves, cascade of shimmering embellishments and figure-skimming cut, the Duchess outshone the assembled super-rich and supermodels. She may have only recently acquired HRH status, but this was an evening which demonstrated that Kate could almost effortlessly blend regal grandeur with laid-back ease.

A month later, this theory was tested against the harsh lens of Hollywood glamour. As part of their first foreign tour, Kate and William landed in Los Angeles to make an impression with the most image-obsessed industry in the world. The pinnacle of the trip was BAFTA's 'Brits to Watch' event, where the Duke and Duchess were arguably the only Brits anyone truly wanted to watch.

With Tom Hanks, Nicole Kidman, Jennifer Lopez and Barbra Streisand among the attendees, there was certainly competition for star quality, but Kate eclipsed them all in a diaphanous lilac gown by Alexander McQueen. The Grecian look was accentuated with a pair of chandelier earrings on loan from the Queen – the kind of bling that money can't buy. Once again, Kate looked relaxed and glowing, exuding the new Cambridge brand of glamour.

**RIGHT** Arriving at a BAFTA event in Los Angeles in July 2011, with Kate wearing a gown by Alexander McQueen.

# BAFTA STYLE

Although her first BAFTA-related appearance was hugely successful, Kate waited until 2017 to begin accompanying Prince William to the annual awards ceremony in London – Britain's answer to the Oscars – which takes place at the Royal Albert Hall each February. The Cambridges are BAFTA's secret weapon, bringing a unique sparkle that no other awards can match. For Kate and William, the BAFTAs are a chance to shine on a global platform, aligning themselves with the glitterati.

However, the BAFTAs have not proven to be a straightforward fashion affair. While in the past, awards ceremonies were simply about pulling off a great look, they've taken on political undertones in recent years, presenting Kate with two of her trickiest wardrobe dilemmas to date.

The relationship between royalty and politics is a delicate one, but there are precedents for managing prime ministers, political posturing and elections. Nevertheless, there was no constitutional guidance for the Duchess of Cambridge when she faced an evening at the BAFTA awards in 2018, the year when the Time's Up movement declared a 'blackout' on the red carpet in protest at sexual discrimination and abuse in the film industry in the wake of the Harvey Weinstein scandal. She was also seven months pregnant at the time.

When she stepped out of her official car, the first camera shots suggested that Kate had indeed opted to show solidarity by wearing black. But once under the spotlights, her Jenny Packham gown was revealed to be a deep bottle green with a black ribbon framing her bump. She finished the look with emerald jewellery, said to signify hope and feminine power. It was the smart, pragmatic choice of a savvy senior royal – while it didn't ignore the evening's theme, it also wasn't a true enough form of protest to make her a poster woman for the campaign. Kate demonstrated impeccable understanding of the balance that would maintain the Royal Family's distance in the long term, rather than seeking short-term gains.

Two years later, there was another fashion storm brewing at the BAFTAs. This time, the focus was on climate change and efforts to make the ceremony eco-friendly. Invitees were sent a guide compiled by the London College of Fashion about how to make sustainable fashion choices. In encouraging A-list actresses to wear something old, BAFTA was somewhat oblivious to the economy of the red carpet, whereby brands pay for the right names to wear their designs. Pulling any old thing out of the wardrobe would have meant actresses jeopardized those relationships and few of them participated in the call to action.

The Duchess, though, had built a reputation on outfit recycling. In the days before the ceremony, Kate fans excitedly debated which gown they would most like to see resurrected. In the end, she made an unexpected choice, arriving in a white and gold Alexander McQueen design first worn during a tour to Malaysia in 2012 (see page 117). It followed the guidelines without requiring the extensive explanation that a vintage piece or design made from specially sourced fabrics might have. With very few actresses following BAFTA's request, the Duchess inadvertently became the evening's eco heroine.

**OPPOSITE** The Duke and Duchess of Cambridge arrive at the 71st British Academy Film Awards at the Royal Albert Hall, February 2018, with Kate in Jenny Packham.

# CLASSIC
# ELEGANCE

**RIGHT** Kate in Alexander McQueen with King Harald of Norway at a dinner held by the Royal Palace on a visit to Norway in 2019.

**OPPOSITE** On a trip to Canada in 2016, Kate chose a Preen dress and shoes by Gianvito Rossi for a reception held at Government House, Victoria, British Columbia.

When dressing for evening engagements, the Duchess's task is apparently simple: be dazzling. More often than not, Kate has stayed true to her style instincts, opting for looks that conform to the tenets of classic, timeless elegance. This approach reinforces her status as a royal who will be on the world stage for years to come. Just as

the Queen's 1950s ball gowns still look romantic and glamorous to us now, so Kate's evening style is designed to look good for years to come.

One moment that perfectly emphasized Kate and William's task of continuity was a dinner held in their honour in Oslo in February 2018, hosted by King Harald and Queen Sonja of Norway.

William spoke at the event of the UK and Norway as 'the strongest of friends', a sentiment that was summed up in the image of the Duchess, pregnant with Prince Louis, on the arm of King Harald almost floating through the hall at the Royal Palace in a frothy pale pink caped McQueen gown. The finishing touch to this stately look was a diamond bracelet given to the Queen by Prince Philip when they married in 1947. In a dress that would have looked right at almost any time over the past 100 years and with nods to both the past and future of the monarchy, the Duchess delivered glamour with gravitas.

When regal sophistication is required, who better for Kate to turn to for inspiration than Grace Kelly? The Hitchcock muse turned Monégasque princess cultivated a personal style that has transcended fashion to become synonymous with exquisite taste. Thus, some of the Duchess's most memorable moments of classic glamour have had something Grace Kelly about them.

For a reception at Government House in Victoria during the Cambridges' 2016 tour to Canada, the Duchess debuted a new bright red dress from British label Preen by Thornton Bregazzi, at once modern and ballerina-chic with its asymmetric neckline, fitted bodice and gently flared box-pleated skirt. These were features reminiscent of the Dior 'New Look'-influenced shapes of the late 1940s and '50s, which Kelly had adopted as her own.

**LEFT** Kate chose Gucci for the annual 100 Women in Finance Gala at the Victoria and Albert Museum in London in February 2019.

**OPPOSITE** Kate wore Erdem to the same Gala Dinner in 2015.

Kate bought the dress on a shopping trip to London department store Fenwick. She clearly agreed with the rest of the world that it was an excellent look, going on to buy the dress in black as well as a similar style in pale blue.

Another Kelly-esque moment came in February 2019, when the Duchess attended the annual 100 Women in Finance Gala, which was raising funds for the Mentally Healthy Schools initiative. This was one of a handful of times she has worn Italian label Gucci, and this bespoke design couldn't have been further from the kooky-eccentric aesthetic of creative director Alessandro Michele.

Instead, this featherweight tulle creation in a palette of rose and dusky pink flowed beautifully. It's a style that Kate had previously worn in similar, darker guises courtesy of Jenny Packham, but the contrasting soft shades of Gucci's version had the edge.

This wasn't a look without controversy, however. The Duchess's decision to show her support to the brand was questioned by many as it was in the throes of a racism row at the time, after releasing a sweater that appeared to recreate blackface. Earlier in the day, Kate had worn a suit by Dolce & Gabbana, which was also in trouble having made a racist advert ahead of a show in China. Though this Gucci gown will look lovely for years to come, its debut was overshadowed by the Duchess's failure to sidestep associations with controversial labels.

# EVENINGWEAR EXPERIMENTS

Timeless elegance might be Kate's comfort zone, but she is not afraid to experiment occasionally, creating a frisson of excitement amid her quintessentially princess looks.

One of her standout forays into statement black tie attire was the maximalist floral gown by

Erdem, chosen for 2015's 100 Women in Finance Gala (see page 125). With its floral pattern and dramatic ruffled skirt, this was more exuberant than almost any other evening look that Kate had tried before – and consequently, it was divisive. But it was a brilliant example of the Duchess

showcasing, undiluted, the talents of one of London Fashion Week's biggest designers with creativity and confidence.

In 2016, Kate added two new names to her evening repertoire, both of them offering her kudos for being trend-conscious. At the Museum of the Year awards in July, the Duchess debuted an off-shoulder dress by Brazilian designer Barbara Casasola, known for her body-conscious, minimalist ethos. This was one of Kate's most daring looks, thanks to its cut-out panelling, and revealed a braver side to her approach than had previously been seen. There was good reason that she might have chosen to wear Casasola, though – this engagement came weeks before the Rio Olympics, so provided a thoughtfully diplomatic gesture of support ahead of the games.

Later in the year, the Duchess showed that she had her finger on the fashion pulse by wearing a dress by Self-Portrait, a label that had become a phenomenon – it was a hit among wedding guests looking for something special at affordable-ish prices. Split to the thigh with a broderie anglaise bodice, Kate's choice – worn for the premiere of *A Street Cat Named Bob* – was proof that she's still in touch with how 'normal' women dress up.

By 2020, Needle & Thread had arguably taken Self-Portrait's place as the contemporary dressing-up brand du jour. Kate gave her support to the unashamedly pretty label when she wore its £410 Aurora dress to the UK-Africa Investment Summit reception at Buckingham Palace. Although the choice was democratic, the effect was nevertheless a masterclass in modern regal style. Demure but covered in sequins, Kate glimmered in every shot taken, while the cherry red shade matched perfectly with the palace's curtains and carpets – and William's tie.

**OPPOSITE LEFT** Kate wears a dress by Brazilian designer Barbara Casasola for the UK Art Fund prize, held at the Natural History Museum in July 2016.

**OPPOSITE RIGHT** Late in the same year, the Duchess wore a Self-Portrait dress to the *A Street Cat Named Bob* film premiere in London.

**ABOVE** In Needle & Thread with Gianvito Rossi heels at Buckingham Palace in January 2020.

# KATE'S
# best of British

The Duchess of Cambridge has always been willing to experiment, lending her sartorial support to a democratically varied mix of brands – a rifle through her wardrobe would reveal dozens of labels, from high street to designer, British and international. She knows that dropping in fresh and surprising names or choosing a designer with a meaningful story to match an engagement will invigorate press interest and offer a chance for fashion flattery.

Kate has two priorities when it comes to her wardrobe: to look impeccable at high-stakes moments and to fly the flag for British fashion.

Despite owning items from a myriad of labels, it was inevitable that the Duchess would need to foster close relationships with an inner circle of designers. Her demands are complex; there is a requirement for complete discretion, an understanding of the sensitivities and dress codes of each event and an awareness of the unique demands on an outfit that will be photographed from every angle in several lights. It's a tall order that can only be met by a handful of the UK's most skilled couturiers.

# ALEXANDER MCQUEEN

After the success of Sarah Burton's wedding dress design for the Duchess of Cambridge, it was inevitable that the two women would continue their collaboration.

Under its eponymous founder, Alexander McQueen was renowned for courting controversy; the autumn/ winter 1995/1996 collection, 'Highland Rape', was a comment on England's historical persecution of Scotland, while in 2001's 'Asylum', self-confessed fat model Michelle Olley lay on a bed of rags wearing a metal mask attached to plastic tubes with butterflies hovering over her naked body. This is the kind of boundary-testing that takes fashion in new directions, but is not, admittedly, the logical starting point for an appropriate Trooping the Colour look for a duchess.

Since McQueen's tragic death in 2010, his right-hand woman Sarah Burton had been reshaping the label, bringing light to its darker corners by exploring the same themes with a softer touch. There was no compromise, however, in the intense artistry that had been integral to the McQueen ethos and was certainly the main draw for Kate in picking the house to make her dress, on the advice of *Vogue*'s then editor Alexandra Shulman.

It was less than two months after the wedding that the Duchess wore McQueen again, choosing a double-breasted coat with gold buttons and epaulettes to present medals to members of the Irish Guards.

The Duchess now has several similar military-style McQueen outfits in her repertoire, but there is huge variety in Sarah Burton's creations. She excels at precise daytime tailoring and there have also been showstopper evening looks, displaying the skills of the McQueen atelier brilliantly.

A handful of times, too, the Duchess has been brave enough to dip her toe into Burton's designs for the McQueen collections presented at fashion weeks, allowing the label to give her a helpful dash of style kudos.

# KATE'S KEY MCQUEEN LOOKS

## The christening of Princess Charlotte, July 2015

The Duchess of Cambridge has worn cream Alexander McQueen for the christening of each of her three children. It was Princess Charlotte's, held at St Mary Magdalene church on the Sandringham Estate that was perhaps the most charming. Kate pushed baby Charlotte in the Silver Cross pram once used by the Queen for her own children as Prince George toddled alongside.

While her McQueen look for George's christening had ruffle detailing, this ivory coat dress was strikingly simple with flat pointed lapels. A flower-strewn Jane Taylor disc hat added dramatic but pretty adornment. Kate clearly loved the coat's clean lines, opting to re-wear it at Trooping the Colour in 2016 and in 2017 at a ceremony to mark the centenary of the Battle of Passchendaele.

In 2018, it became the focus of a royal fashion mystery. Three weeks after Prince Louis's birth, the Duchess wore what seemed to be the same coat to the wedding of Prince Harry and Meghan Markle. However, eagle-eyed royal watchers noted that the new coat had a row of buttons at the sleeve and was pale yellow. Kate could not have been accused of attempting to upstage Meghan with a new look, quite simply recreating one she already loved. Later, she also wore the same coat in blue.

**OPPOSITE** The Duchess chose a cream Alexander McQueen coat dress for Princess Charlotte's christening in 2015.

## Red for The Queen's Diamond Jubilee River Pageant, June 2012

If you were in any doubt about the level of consideration involved in masterminding royal looks, you need only refer to the outfits concocted for the pageant that took place in June 2012 to celebrate 60 years since the Queen had ascended the throne.

The Queen's own white outfit was embellished with silver, gold and crystal discs to reflect each of her jubilee celebrations. The Duchess of Cambridge would have been keen to be seen, but also at pains not to upstage Her Majesty. Red, then, was a considered choice that stood out in arrivals pictures yet blended perfectly with the red and gold Spirit of Chartwell barge that carried the Royal Family down the River Thames. This is an early example of the sleek dress designs that McQueen has made multiple times for the Duchess, becoming almost a uniform.

Kate added thoughtful touches to include other UK and Commonwealth countries in her look, wearing a maple leaf hat debuted in Canada the previous year and carrying a scarf in Strathearn tartan, a nod to her and William's Scottish titles, the Earl and Countess of Strathearn.

## Red and white in Vancouver, 2016

When the Duchess of Cambridge appeared in this red and white tiered dress in Vancouver on the first day of her Canadian tour in 2016, it was one of her boldest daytime looks to date.

The bespoke design was adapted from Sarah Burton's Resort 2017 range – Kate had obviously been afforded a preview. McQueen's creative director cited a very British set of inspirations for the collection, drawing on the hand-painted motifs found on canal barges and gypsy caravans. Yet the red and white colour palette still gave a diplomatic nod to the Duchess's hosts. Kate finished

**ABOVE LEFT** The Duchess of Cambridge wears Alexander McQueen for the Diamond Jubilee Pageant in 2012.

**LEFT** Arriving in Vancouver on the first leg of a Canada tour in 2017, Kate wears a red and white tiered dress from Alexander McQueen Resort 2017.

the look off with matching bright red Russell & Bromley heels and a Miu Miu clutch bag.

## LBD in Paris, 2017

In the capital of chic, the Duchess of Cambridge simply had to wear a Little Black Dress. Rather than opting for Chanel (that would come the following day), the label that coined the iconic garment, Kate enlisted Sarah Burton to create a Duchess-proof take on the classic style.

Burton excelled herself with this tweed fit-and-flare design that hovered elegantly just above the ankles. Kate finished the look with pearl Balenciaga earrings and a matching ring and necklace – the effect was quintessentially Parisian.

It wasn't just classic elegance that Kate pulled off in this McQueen look. As Alexander McQueen is a British label with a British creative director but owned by French conglomerate Kering, it also encapsulated the highest echelons of British and French fashion on a trip that was all about cementing cultural ties ahead of Brexit.

## State banquet for the King and Queen of the Netherlands, October 2018

As Kate sought to update her style after the birth of Prince Louis, so Burton and McQueen adjusted with her. This lilac gown, created for a state banquet celebrating the King and Queen of the Netherlands' visit to the UK, was bolder than any the Duchess had tried before.

The silk taffeta dress managed to look at once modern and traditional, with its fishtail skirt, delicate pleats and rosebud decoration. It more than held its own with Kate's fabulous jewels and regalia, which included the Lover's Knot tiara, Princess Alexandra's pearl and diamond necklace and the Royal Family Order, a personal honour awarded by the Queen.

**ABOVE RIGHT** Wearing a McQueen LBD at the British Embassy in Paris in March 2017.

**RIGHT** Kate in a silk taffeta gown by Alexander McQueen at a state banquet at Buckingham Palace for the King and Queen of the Netherlands in October 2018.

# CATHERINE WALKER & CO

Catherine Walker's name will, of course, forever be associated with Princess Diana. The mother-in-law the Duchess of Cambridge never met forged an early friendship with the French-born designer, and began wearing her clothes while pregnant with Prince William. Walker evolved with the Princess, dressing her for every phase of her style journey, from the polka dot dresses of the early 1980s to slick cocktail frocks in the '90s. Diana was even buried in a black Catherine Walker dress.

Although Catherine herself had passed away by the time Kate required a public wardrobe, the relationship between the Chelsea-based couturier and this new generation of the Royal family remained strong. Carole Middleton wore a Catherine Walker & Co outfit for William and Kate's wedding, and her daughter placed her first order for her tour to Canada in 2011.

Now designed by Walker's husband Said Cyrus, the label specializes in the exquisite tailoring and thoughtful designs that the Duchess requires. Although there was a hiatus of three years between Kate's first and second Catherine Walker looks, she now relies heavily on the label for perfectly cut tour outfits and occasion-appropriate coat dresses. The label's understated, personal service is a highly valued asset.

## Lilac skirt suit in the Netherlands, 2017

The Duchess of Cambridge had a Jackie Kennedy moment courtesy of Said Cyrus on her maiden solo overseas trip in 2017. The first in a series of Brexit 'charm offensives', the Royal Family's most glamorous asset was dispatched to the Netherlands. And who

**RIGHT** The Duchess of Cambridge on a trip to the Netherlands in October 2017, wearing a lilac skirt suit by Catherine Walker & Co.

**OPPOSITE ABOVE** In a Catherine Walker & Co coat dress worn with praline Gianvito Rossi pumps at the Commonwealth War Graves Tyne Cot Cemetary in July 2017.

better to emulate on this mission of soft diplomacy than America's most famous, trend setting First Lady?

With its nipped waist, rolled-collar jacket and neat pencil skirt, the look cast Kate as a sophisticated yet businesslike ambassador. It's a testament to the atelier, too, that the suit survived the flight uncreased.

## Coat dress in Belgium, 2017

Catherine Walker's designs have, on occasion, been accused of being too 'old' for the Duchess. They may not be the kinds of pieces your average 30-something might choose, but Kate's requirements are singular and the label's coat dresses are perfect when a stately look is required. On a visit to Belgium to mark commemorations of the First World War's bloodiest battles, the Duchess's pale grey coat dress was sombre and respectful, with its delicate leaf pattern adding a sense of softness.

## Turquoise in Pakistan, 2019

Diana, Princess of Wales often turned to Catherine Walker to create her tour wardrobes, entrusting her to include flattering fashion messages – such as the gown she made for the Princess's visit to Saudi Arabia in 1986, embellished with a cast of falcons flying down its train in tribute to the birds, which are so highly prized in the kingdom. The Duchess of Cambridge harnessed this expertise for her visit to Pakistan in 2019. One of the most impactful looks of the tour was the anarkali-inspired dress and trousers that Kate wore to land in Islamabad. The design included a draped neckline as a nod to the dupatta scarf worn as part of traditional Pakistani dress. It was meaningful that the Duchess worked with Cyrus on pieces for the tour, as his Persian background is an added reminder of British links to Asia.

**RIGHT** Arriving in Pakistan in October 2019 wearing Catherine Walker & Co with Rupert Sanderson cream heels.

# JENNY PACKHAM

When William and Kate's engagement was announced, Jenny Packham was one of the frontrunners to create the bridal gown. In the end, the Duchess made a bolder choice, but Packham has still become a favoured designer, charged with making each of Kate's 'leaving hospital' looks after the births of her babies (see pages 107–109), as well as many evening and formal occasion ensembles.

## *Yellow dress in Calgary, 2011*

One of the first dresses that Packham created for the Duchess of Cambridge will be remembered for what courtiers might consider to be all the wrong reasons. Kate suffered a 'Marilyn' moment at Calgary Airport when her Jenny Packham dress (see page 129) was swept up by a gust of wind. In many ways, it added to the new Duchess's fresh glamour as she undertook her first tour, but it's a scenario the Queen has always sought to avoid by having weights placed in the hems of her skirts.

**ABOVE** The Duchess of Cambridge wears Jenny Packham at the Team GB Gala at the Royal Albert Hall in May 2012.

**RIGHT** The Duke and Duchess of Cambridge with Prince George and Princess Charlotte arrive in Canada in September 2016. Kate is wearing a Jenny Packham dress, a Lock & Co. hat and Gianvito Rossi pumps.

## Teal gown, 2012

Jenny Packham played a starring role in cultivating Kate's 'princess' image in the early years of her marriage, providing modern fairytale gowns that flattered the new Duchess but never made her look too 'fashion'. An excellent case in point was this soft, flowing teal creation, which Kate wore to a gala at the Royal Albert Hall celebrating Team GB ahead of the London Olympics. With its pleated chiffon skirt, delicate lace back and shoulders and décolletage-baring cut, the Duchess looked youthfully regal – not an easy combination to master, but Packham's skilful balance of daring and classical glamour made it possible.

The dress was such a hit that Kate wore it again in 2018 to the Tusk Conservation Awards.

## Arriving in Canada, 2016

Being part of big Cambridge family moments has become a cornerstone of Jenny Packham's contribution to the Duchess's wardrobe. This was underscored when she created Kate's look to land in Canada at the beginning of the family's first tour as a foursome after Princess Charlotte's arrival.

The Duchess opted for a sleek shift dress with structured shoulders and a neat pointed collar. The royal blue colour acknowledged the flag of British Columbia and was a theme echoed by everyone in the family, from William's tie to George's sweater and Charlotte's dress and shoes.

Packham's design was complemented by Kate's Lock & Co. hat, featuring maple leaf decorations.

## More of Kate's best-loved British designers...

EMILIA WICKSTEAD New Zealand-born designer Emilia Wickstead has made modern sophistication her calling card and gathered a global crowd of fans who adore the feminine simplicity of her designs. For Kate, they offer demure but striking options for everything from church services to charity visits.

ERDEM Known for his romantic aesthetic and painterly florals, Erdem Moralioglu has been a favourite of the Duchess's from the beginning; she wore his navy lace dress to alight from the plane at the start of her first tour in 2011. Erdem has carved a niche in unashamedly pretty pieces that are perfect for day and evening engagements alike.

ALICE TEMPERLEY Even before she married William, the Duchess of Cambridge had zoned in on Alice Temperley's bohemian, decorative designs. Shortly after her engagement, Kate wore a white chiffon dress with black embroidery to attend a fundraiser with her new fiancé. Ever since, Temperley has brought the bucolic inspiration of her Somerset upbringing to the royal wardrobe, providing intricately patterned pieces that are special and feminine.

ROKSANDA Roksanda Ilincic, who came to London from her native Belgrade to study at Central Saint Martins in 1999, has brought a zingy palette and architectural silhouettes to London Fashion Week. Kate has deployed her Roksanda purchases to introduce exciting colour-blocking and out-of-the-ordinary cuts to her clothing collection.

MULBERRY The Duchess has worn several Mulberry dresses and coats over the past 10 years as well as snapping up its bags. Thanks to its British-with-a-hint-of-kitsch look, the label adds a subtle sense of fun to Kate's style – see the crystal-button coat she wore to inspect the Scouts in 2013, or the fuchsia coat worn in New York in 2014.

# JEWELLERY
# & accessories

The Duchess of Cambridge's clothing may make an instant visual impact, but
the stories woven through her jewellery and accessories are just as intriguing.
They create a narrative reflecting Kate's journey through life from girlfriend
to wife to mother, or underlining her role as a representative of Queen and
country, as well as a mother, wife and daughter-in-law of future sovereigns.

As with the rest of her wardrobe, the Duchess takes a high/low approach to accessories. During a visit to Ireland in 2020, she segued from £17,000 diamond Asprey studs by day to £6 hoops from H&M by night. It's a transition few women make naturally, but Kate's determination to do so highlights her efforts to be both regal and in touch.

'Prince William is very sweet and kind and spoils me,' Kate once told a little girl who asked her what it was like to be a princess. It's an assertion backed up by the easy rapport that the couple share in public, but also by the precious pieces of jewellery that have emerged over the years, from Princess Diana's sapphire earrings (which match that famous engagement ring) to Kiki McDonough amethyst and diamond earrings to mark their first Christmas as a married couple

to a Cartier Ballon Bleu watch, thought to have been a 'push' present following the arrival of Prince George, and a slim diamond eternity ring that sits between the Duchess's wedding and engagement bands.

These are tokens that offer an outward, traditional display of love and commitment, yet nestled among these are pieces that speak to the Duchess's public role and fashion awareness.

Accessories have the power to make or break an outfit, but also to transform it. Often, it is not the clothes that the Duchess has chosen, but how she elects to style them that is truly significant. A new shoe or bag revives old favourites or can switch an ensemble from casual to elevated and vice versa, while the right brooch can take an outfit from meaningless to meaningful.

**RIGHT** The Duchess of Cambridge updates a purple skirt suit with an Aspinal bag and Rupert Sanderson heels on a visit to the Royal Opera House in London in January 2019.

**OPPOSITE** In an Alexander McQueen coat dress and a Jane Taylor hat at a ceremony to mark the 100th anniversary of the First World War in Liège, Belgium, August 2014.

When Kate was attending Olympic events in 2012, for which she evidently decided that 'smart yet sporty' was her modus operandi, she would offset casual skinny jeans with sky-high wedges. It may not have been a look to the taste of fashion insiders, but it served to tick all the boxes required of her position as a royal ambassador.

Later, in 2019, Kate hinted at a reinvigorated style outlook as she eased back into work after giving birth to Prince Louis by re-wearing an Oscar de la Renta skirt suit and lending it a new fashion edge by adding an of-the-moment Aspinal box bag and decorative gold-buckled Rupert

Sanderson heels in lieu of her usual pared-back, 'safe' accoutrements. Updating an outfit with trophy accessories is a fashion tip as old as time, but for a Duchess whose image is so carefully cultivated, this was an important signal of a new chapter – both sartorially and professionally.

Even before that, though, the Duchess's accessories had evolved along with her role and priorities. Her early royal years were defined by subtle items that were elegant and fail-safe – what they lacked in flair, they made up for in all-important appropriateness. Neutral shades and streamlined silhouettes that go with everything

were typical, with statement pieces
kept to a minimum.

A look into Kate's shoe cupboard
would reveal dozens of sleek heels
in plush suedes and buttery leathers.
Her early commitment to anything
on the 'nude' spectrum is legendary,
perhaps thanks to their streamlining,
leg-lengthening effect and ability to
match anything. She owns around 30
variations of shoes in this colour palette
– mostly courts from Russell & Bromley,
Gianvito Rossi, L.K. Bennett and Emmy
London, but there are also strappy
sandals and espadrille wedges.

Meanwhile, Kate was dedicated
to neat box and envelope clutch bags,
which are small enough to carry the
tiny number of essentials she might
require (perhaps some tissues and a
tube of her favourite Clarins lip gloss)
yet substantial enough to carry out
their most important task – giving royal
hands something to do. The Duchess
may not have veered quite into handbag-
signalling territory like the Queen
(who supposedly uses her bag to send
messages to her ladies-in-waiting: by
placing her bag on the table she is saying
she wishes to leave in five minutes, while
a handbag on the floor signifies that
she wishes to be rescued from her
conversation), but her collection of
clutches is useful for looking natural
in photographs. Mulberry, Alexander
McQueen, L.K. Bennett and Emmy
London are Kate's top purveyors of
diminutive hand occupiers.

**LEFT** The Duchess arriving at the Wimbledon Championships in 2017, wearing a polka dot Dolce & Gabbana dress with open-toe sandals from Office and a Victoria Beckham tote bag.

**OPPOSITE** At the King's Cup Regatta in May 2019 wearing block-heel shoes and clutch bag both by Emmy London.

We may have assumed that the Duchess might settle into a signature combination of pale heels plus mini clutch with the potential to become as iconic as the Queen's Launer top-handle bag and Anello & Davide block heel, but she has latterly developed more adventurous accessory ideas.

The debut of a pair of checked and tasseled J.Crew heels during a Canada visit in 2016 felt like a turning point. In 2017, there were the glittery Oscar de la Renta heels (which drew instant comparisons to Cinderella's glass slippers). And at that year's Wimbledon Championships, Kate chose to style her polka dot Dolce & Gabbana dress with a large white leather Victoria Beckham handbag (what could she have been carrying in there?) and black strappy sandals by high-street label Office. This was also the day that she revealed a shorter, choppier hairstyle. Everything came together to create a modern, glossy feel.

As well as adding these noteworthy pieces, the Duchess was evolving her familiar coterie with more nuanced updates. An early tendency to wear beloved boots and shoes over and over until they were looking a little bit scuffed was out, and clever tonal variations of her favourite shapes were in. This approach is exemplified by the block-heel navy Josie pumps (sturdier than stilettos, but chicer than wedges) and scarlet clutch, both by Emmy London, worn to the launch of the King's Cup Regatta in May 2019, or the way Kate offset her red riding coat with rich burgundy velvet Jimmy Choos at Westminster Abbey in March 2020.

In tandem with Kate's first decade as a Duchess, a revolution has happened in fashion that has seen sales of heels plummet as women embrace flat shoes and trainers. As a royal required to dress formally and facing the prospect of being photographed from every angle at every

engagement, Kate has not been as quick as many to abandon heels, but she has incorporated more flats into her repertoire.

During the visit to Pakistan in October 2019, she wore Russell & Bromley's crossover flats in both blush and black. A few months later, Kate tapped into the trainer trend by wearing a bright white, striped £29.50 pair by M&S to a SportsAid event. The retailer had only recently expanded its range of fashionable sneakers to cater to growing demand, which can only have been accelerated by backing from the UK's most style-conscious royal.

# THE TIARAS

One time that the Duchess of Cambridge is truly not like the rest of us is when she dons a tiara. These are rare occasions but, unsurprisingly, they are awaited with great excitement by royal fans, who delight in these moments of regal grandeur.

After borrowing the Queen's Cartier Halo tiara on her wedding day, it was more than four years before the Duchess was seen in public view wearing one again (shots taken through a car window in 2013 showed only a hint). It was fitting that the future Queen's first major tiara moment came at a state banquet in honour of one of Buckingham Palace's most important visitors of recent times, President Xi Jinping of China.

For the dinner in October 2015, the Duchess was seated beside the guest of honour dressed in a look replete with opulence and meticulous diplomatic details. Her Jenny Packham gown was red, the most important colour in Chinese culture and a signal of luck, happiness and good fortune

for her guest. She had also selected the Lotus Flower tiara, a piece created by Garrard for the Queen Mother in the 1920s but appropriately incorporating a flower synonymous with China. Kate's first state banquet look was finished off with diamond earrings and two bracelets, also on loan from the Queen.

The Lotus Flower tiara has remained in the vaults since and the Duchess exclusively wears the Cambridge Lover's Knot tiara instead. Bigger and bolder than the Lotus Flower, the Duchess has been photographed in this exquisite pearl and diamond creation on eight occasions.

Not only is the tiara's Cambridge name a fitting reference to Kate's title, but also it was often worn by Princess Diana, who was loaned the heirloom by the Queen around the time of her marriage. The piece, which includes 19 baroque pearl pendants, was created in 1913 by Garrard for Queen Mary, who sought to emulate a tiara owned by her grandmother Augusta, who had become Duchess of Cambridge when she married Prince Adolphus, the Duke of Cambridge (and cousin of Queen Victoria) in 1818.

Although Diana is said to have complained that the tiara was heavy and gave her a headache, the Duchess of Cambridge has not, to public knowledge, made any such protestations and has now made the Cambridge Lover's Knot famous for a new generation of tiara aficionados.

# THE L.K. BENNETT SLEDGE

**RIGHT** The Duchess of Cambridge in Adelaide, Australia in April 2014 wearing an Alexander McQueen dress plus L.K. Bennett Sledge heels.

**OPPOSITE** Kate in an Alexander McQueen dress with L.K. Bennett Sledge heels and a Prada clutch for the Queen's Diamond Jubilee Service of Thanksgiving at St Paul's Cathedral, June 2012.

If there is one item in Kate's wardrobe that epitomizes her early years as a Duchess, then it has to be L.K. Bennett's £195 patent beige Sledge heels. Ask any bystander the first piece that comes to mind when they think of Kate's style, and these heels are sure to be a popular answer.

The Sledges had their maiden royal outing on 4 June 2011, when the Duchess wore them to the Epsom Derby. Her decision to choose shoes that matched her skin tone was not groundbreaking; Coleen Rooney, Victoria Beckham and Angelina Jolie were just a few of the women who had already landed on the 'nude' shoe's power to elongate and elevate, as well as match any look. But the style had really arrived once Kate backed it, and when she wore the L.K. Bennetts eight more times within eight weeks of that first appearance, she had made the style her own.

Some loved the endearingly thrifty practicality that Kate's newfound shoe penchant exhibited; others were exasperated by her apparent inability to experiment. 'Does Kate only own ONE pair of shoes?' protested *Mail on Sunday* columnist Liz Jones in June 2012, by which time Kate had worn them on a total of 13 occasions.

Undeterred, Kate's Sledges were seen another 21 times, including repeatedly during a tour to Singapore and Malaysia and in New Zealand and Australia, before they were retired in August 2014. Fittingly, they made their final appearance, after 34 wears, at a cemetery in Belgium, where the Duchess commemorated the centenary of the beginning of the First World War.

Kate had transformed a high-street shoe into a piece of fashion history. In 2015, the Victoria and Albert Museum, of which Kate is patron, acquired a pair of Sledges in acknowledgment of their important place in the style canon.

'When it became apparent that nude court heels were a wardrobe staple of the Duchess of Cambridge, sales rocketed,' the shoes' museum label reads. 'The popularity of the shoe showed that emulating royal fashion is a practice unchanged since at least Queen Henrietta Maria's time.'

Although the Sledges – which are still available to buy at L.K. Bennett – have not been seen again on the Duchess, she still loves heels in skin-complementing shades; Gianvito Rossi's 105 praline suede pumps have been seen 24 times. But it will be hard for any shoe to match the enduring notoriety of the Sledge.

**LEFT** On her first solo overseas visit to the Netherlands in 2016, Kate wore a pair of pearl and diamond earrings loaned to her by the Queen.

**OPPOSITE** In a Stella McCartney dress and Cartier gold hoop necklace at the National Portrait Gallery in 2012.

# JEWELLERY WITH MEANING

For centuries, jewellery has been about more than mere adornment. For women and men the world over, the decorations they wear offer signs of who they are, how they wish to be seen and what they have achieved.

So it is for the Duchess of Cambridge, whose collection of jewellery spans from sweet acknowledgments of her love for her children to family treasures that not only tell her own story, but that of the Windsor dynasty.

It is not all truly her own, of course. Kate also has numerous items that are on long-term loan from the Queen, having reportedly made an ally of Angela Kelly, the Queen's wardrobe advisor and personal dresser, who is in charge of the royal jewellery vaults.

Some of Kate's most familiar pieces of jewellery appear only in certain contexts. They have been passed down through generations of the Royal Family and will continue to be worn by different women for years to come. For all engagements related to the Irish Guards, for example, Kate wears a simple but beautiful shamrock brooch that is traditionally loaned to royals who perform ceremonial duties for the regiment. In New Zealand in 2014, the Duchess became the first person to borrow a platinum and diamond fern (silver fern are endemic to the country) brooch from the Queen, who originally received it as a Christmas gift from the women of Auckland during her visit in 1953.

Similarly, the Queen's father, King George VI, gave his wife a diamond maple leaf brooch to mark their state visit to Canada in 1939. Since the Queen Mother's death in 2002, the Queen, the Duchess of Cornwall and now Kate wear this sentimental piece whenever they visit the Commonwealth nation.

A more unexpected example of the Duchess borrowing pieces from the Queen's collection came in 2016, when Kate undertook her first solo trip abroad to The Hague. One of her stops was a visit to the Mauritshuis to view an exhibition of paintings by Vermeer, among them the famous *Girl with a Pearl Earring*. Kate lingered by the artwork so that photographers could capture her delicate pearl and diamond drop earrings, on loan from the Queen, beside the style that inspired the book and film starring Scarlett Johansson.

Other spectacular pieces owned by Her Majesty that Kate wears include the Cartier diamond drop necklace the Queen chose as a wedding gift from the Nizam of Hyderabad, a pair of sapphire and diamond drop earrings that once belonged to the Queen Mother and a diamond bracelet that was once Queen Mary's choker.

**LEFT** Kate's Cartier Ballon Bleu wristwatch teamed with the Art Deco diamond earrings and bracelet set given to her as a wedding gift by her father-in-law, the Prince of Wales.

The Duchess has incorporated pieces from Princess Diana's collection into her own, a gesture that gives the jewellery new life and includes the late Princess in the story of a new generation. To complement her heirloom engagement ring, William gave Kate his mother's sapphire and diamond earrings as a wedding gift, which she remodelled into a simple drop style that she has been wearing since 2011. She has two sets of pearl earrings that were favourites of Diana; the

**ABOVE** On a visit to The Ely & Caerau Children's Centre in Cardiff, Wales in January 2020, the Duchess wore a gold pendant by Daniella Draper inscribed with the initials of her children's names.

Collingwood pair were a wedding gift to the Princess from the jewellers and were first worn by the Duchess to a state banquet for the King and Queen of Spain in 2017, while the opulent diamond and South Sea pearl earrings, with their distinctive C-shaped sweep of diamonds, were worn by Kate to the BAFTAs in 2019. Then there is the triple-strand pearl bracelet – originally created by Nigel Milne in 1988 and sold in aid of the charity Birthright, of which the Diana was patron – that Kate revived for a reception in Germany in 2017.

Prince Charles and the Duchess of Cornwall have given Kate pieces, too. An Art Deco suite, including a bracelet, ring and earrings incorporating yellow and white diamonds, is believed to have been a wedding gift from William's father, while the Duchess wore a chunky gold charm bracelet with C inscriptions on each side – one for Catherine, the other for Camilla – to Wimbledon in 2011.

Though it's always noteworthy when the Duchess chooses to wear a meaningful piece of jewellery, there are occasions that stand out. She owns several pieces from Cartier's Trinity collection, which is distinguished by its bands of white, rose and yellow gold. The first piece that Kate was photographed wearing from the range was a £49,000 necklace featuring five hoops on a gold chain that she wore to view portraits of Team GB at the National Portrait Gallery ahead of the 2012 Olympic Games (see page 149), with royal press officers explaining that, 'it's a personal piece. It's not an official Olympic item, but it's appropriate to wear it'. A statement that did little to quell astonishment at the price tag.

It is Kate's role as a mother that has brought some of her sweetest and most simple jewellery gestures. A few months after Prince George's birth, the Duchess was photographed wearing a charm necklace bearing her son's full name. It was later revealed that the £89 design, from a boutique site called Merci Maman, had been given to Kate by her sister Pippa. While she never wore that necklace on official business, the Duchess did decide that the time was right to use jewellery to keep her children close in early 2020 when she was launching her most high-profile solo initiative to date, the Five Big Questions survey about childhood. For a visit to a children's centre in Wales and a women's prison in Surrey, she wore a £1,000 pendant by British jeweller Daniella Draper inscribed with the letters G, C, L, plus three stars. The necklace served to illustrate the motivation for a work project into which she has poured so much enthusiasm – it would have made a great icebreaker when speaking to nervous parents, too.

**ABOVE** Kate sporting a navy-blue dress and a Zara jewelled hairband at the Royal British Legion Festival of Remembrance in 2019.

## HATS AND HATBANDS

Elegantly sculptural hats have, naturally, become a mainstay of the Duchess of Cambridge's official wardrobe. The Royal Family has long been credited for the UK's vibrant millinery industry; not only do royal women make excellent ambassadors for the artistry of milliners, but the events to which they lend their presence fuel demand, from garden parties at the palaces to Royal Ascot.

Kate settled on a hat style signature early on, and while she has added numerous designs to her arsenal since then, the simple premise of each purchase has remained similar. The Duchess loves discs, saucers and, occasionally, pillboxes that sit jauntily on top of the head, adding height and decorative flamboyance via bows, twists, netting, silk petals and ribbons, while still allowing for a complex updo and not obscuring her face in any way. One of her go-to creatives is Jane Taylor, who describes her style as 'timeless, elegant yet forward thinking'. Then there's Sylvia Fletcher of Lock & Co., whose creations are a little more traditional but still full of flair, Jane Corbett, who combines prettiness with artful shaping, and Philip Treacy, who brings fashionable exuberance.

'I'm so honoured to design and make pieces for the Duchess,' confides Taylor. 'We design specifically for the client and know these pieces are worn to very special occasions, so must be perfect. All the team are passionate about using traditional techniques to create heirloom pieces that will be enjoyed by generations. Seeing these pieces in the press at such important occasions is a highlight for us all.'

Millinery may appear to be a fashion sector that evolves at a glacial pace, but the Duchess helped to create a seismic shift when she opted to wear a 'hatband' for the christening of Prince Louis in June 2018. Akin to an oversized Alice band and sometimes called a Boleyn band (because the second wife of King Henry VIII wore a similar headpiece), the Duchess sparked a trend for an accessory that last enjoyed the fashion spotlight in the era of the Sloane Ranger and made a calculated effort to be the heroine of its resurgence that year, wearing a blue floral take to the wedding of her friend Sophie Carter and a pumped-up green velvet version at Westminster Abbey.

**ABOVE** The Duchess chose Erdem and a Jane Corbett hat for Trooping the Colour, June 2012.

**RIGHT** Arriving in Dublin for a three-day tour of Ireland in March 2020. Kate wears a Catherine Walker & Co coat, an Alessandra Rich dress and a padded velvet headband.

In Alexander McQueen with a Jane Taylor hatband and Cassandra Goad pearl studs at the christening of Prince Louis in July 2018.

Jane Taylor explains that her hatband had mystical inspirations beyond the historical. 'The headband or crescent moon shape was a mix of inspiration from Indian gods and goddesses,' she says. 'The moon is such a feminine symbol and I wanted to bring this into my work.'

Tastemaker extraordinaire Miuccia Prada featured padded satin headbands in her spring/summer 2019 show. Had one of fashion's most avant-garde designers been influenced by the Duchess? Kate made sure that the world was reminded that she was queen of the hatband, sporting a new plush red iteration for Christmas at Sandringham and a fabulous feathered coral band for the christening of Harry and Meghan's son Archie in the summer of 2019.

Later in 2019, the Duchess seemed to nod to her own influence by wearing a jewelled hairband by Zara to the Festival of Remembrance – a piece that had probably been made in response to demand she had had a part in fuelling. Accessible, ladylike and with a reference to one of England's historic queens, there could hardly be a more perfect accessory for Kate to have made her own.

## The Duchess's favourite jeweller: Kiki McDonough

Although Kate's jewellery collection comprises pieces of all origins and budgets, she returns again and again to fine jeweller Kiki McDonough. She owns 21 sets of earrings and two necklaces, ranging from delicate diamond studs to colourful, timeless drop designs incorporating gems including amethyst, tourmaline, topaz, citrine and more.

'My ethos has always been to design jewellery that people can wear as often as possible,' says McDonough. 'I remember when my father – who was an antique jeweller – brought home some amazing pieces. We admired them, but I used to look at them and think that I would never wear them, which seemed rather a waste.'

These observations inspired the philosophy that is fundamental to her own jewellery. 'I decided to base all my designs on my lifestyle. At work I would dress to go to meetings and events. Outside of work I was a busy mother who also went to watch football matches, to supper with friends and to parties,' she reflects. 'Many of my designs I put on at the beginning of the week and will still be wearing on Friday.'

McDonough, whose jewellery was also worn by Princess Diana, pinpoints the appeal of her designs for the Duchess of Cambridge, whose own schedule includes a huge variety of scenarios. 'The Duchess has worn my jewellery for a number of different occasions, ranging from formal events to playing on the sports field,' she reflects. 'I hope that for all my clients the pieces work well and make them feel pretty when they are at home with family and when they have a special occasion to dress up for. It is not bling or cutting edge, but it adds a touch of colour and brightens the face.'

'When I see the Duchess of Cambridge wearing my pieces, of course I am incredibly flattered,' adds McDonough, 'but more importantly I am pleased that it fits in with her busy life as a working mother.'

# channelling DIANA

Diana, Princess of Wales was a fashion icon whose calculated style
evolution traced the dramatic tale of her life, from aristocratic virgin
bride to dazzling princess to wronged wife to independent modern
woman. Her legend is unique and irreplaceable.

Yet it would undoubtedly have been essential for Kate, William and their advisors to ensure that, while they honoured Diana's memory, the new Duchess of Cambridge – who would one day become Princess of Wales and then Queen – carved her own path.

Indeed, there was plenty of history that the Cambridges were keen not to repeat. 'I'm trying to learn from lessons done in the past and I just wanted to give her the best chance to settle in and to see what happens on the other side,' William said in the couple's engagement interview with Tom Bradby, referring to his mother's rapid transformation from Sloane Ranger nanny to Prince Charles' fiancée.

Anna Harvey, the *Vogue* editor who helped dress Diana throughout her public life, also expressed some regret at helping to raise the Princess's international profile with fashion.

'It got out of control, I think, and none of us saw the danger,' she told *The Telegraph*.

As this book exemplifies, the Duchess of Cambridge has not shied away from the powerful tool that fashion can be, but her approach has been more gentle and often less personal, focusing on wider themes of diplomacy, relatability and being an ambassador for British fashion.

The Duchess has navigated the first decade of royal life in her own way, but comparisons with her late mother-in-law's style are inevitable. In part, that's because Diana's repertoire was vast – most of us could find a picture to match what we're wearing right now with an outfit the Princess once wore, whether that be jeans and a t-shirt, a trouser suit or evening dress. But there have been moments when similarities between Kate's latest look and a Diana fashion reference seemed, if not intentional, then touchingly appropriate.

## THE STRAPLESS VELVET GOWN

One of Diana's earliest fashion faux pas was a strapless black taffeta gown by the Emanuels, which she wore to a charity gala in London soon after her engagement to Prince Charles. She'd chosen the dress from the designers' sample rail and it hadn't been fitted to her figure, meaning that she was rather over-exposed as she exited the car. 'Daring Di sets fashion as she takes the plunge,' read one headline the next day. There were also raised eyebrows at the palace that she had chosen black, usually a colour reserved for mourning attire, even if it was a glamorous choice beyond the constraints of royal protocol.

Kate chose a similar gown for *The Sun* Military Awards in December 2011. Flanked by William and Harry, she wore a strapless black velvet creation by Alexander McQueen that clearly fitted impeccably. The look was finished with a set of diamond and ruby jewellery she'd received as a wedding gift. Visually there might have been echoes of Diana's 1981 look, but the mood couldn't have been more different.

## THE FLORAL PUSSY-BOW DRESS

On the 20th anniversary of Diana's death, William, Harry and Kate visited the Princess Diana Memorial Garden in the grounds of Kensington Palace. For this Diana-centric appearance, comparisons were bound to be made, and Kate embraced this by choosing a floral pussy-bow Prada tea dress that could have been pulled from the late Princess's early '80s wardrobe. The pattern incorporated poppies, a fitting symbol of remembrance.

It was perhaps extra special that this was the Duchess's last public outing before it was announced that she was pregnant with her third child, Prince Louis.

**OPPOSITE ABOVE**
Princess Diana in a black
taffeta Emanuel gown at
her first public engagement
at the Royal Opera House,
London, 1981.

**OPPOSITE BELOW**
Princess Diana in a blue
floral dress leaving her
wedding rehearsal, 1981.

**RIGHT** Kate in a floral-
print Prada dress on
a visit to the Princess
Diana Memorial Garden
in Kensington Gardens,
August 2017.

**OPPOSITE** Kate in a Maheen Khan teal shalwar kameez on the Cambridges' trip to Pakistan in October 2019.

**RIGHT** Princess Diana arriving at Lahore Hospital, Pakistan wearing a similarly coloured shalwar kameez in May 1997.

# THE SHALWAR KAMEEZ

One of Diana's most famous final fashion moments came during her visit to Pakistan in 1997. Ostensibly, she was there to visit her friends Imran and Jemima Khan, but she had an ulterior motive: winning over the family of Hasnat Khan, the heart surgeon with whom she was in love. Her wardrobe of beautifully decorative shalwar kameezes was a huge hit, both in Pakistan and around the world.

Twenty-two years later, Kate and William's visit to Pakistan was always going to revive memories of the time the Prince's mother had spent in the country. In India, three years before, Kate had been reluctant to embrace traditional dress, but here she excelled herself with several looks by local designers, many of which mirrored the colour and details of Diana's Pakistan wardrobe.

# THE NAVY GOWN

Kate's eveningwear has settled into a comfortable theme of being pretty, delicate and glamorous. But for 2019's Diplomatic Reception, she upped the ante in one of the most dramatic formal looks she has ever worn – a long-sleeved, midnight blue velvet concoction by Alexander McQueen.

With its pointed shoulders and sweetheart neckline, the dress showed the Duchess playing with silhouette as never before. It also bore notable similarities to one of Diana's most famous dresses – the Victor Edelstein gown she had worn to dance with John Travolta at the White House in 1985, described by Eleri Lynn, curator at Historic Royal Palaces (and keeper of a vast collection of royal clothes from history), as 'a key moment in the story of 20th-century royal fashion.'

The dress's place in fashion history was assured when it broke the record for a garment sold in auction at Christie's sale of Diana's wardrobe in 1997, fetching $225,000. In the same week that Kate wore the velvet McQueen, Diana's dress was up for sale again, eventually being snapped up by HRP for its archives.

# THE POLKA DOT DRESS

Polka dots were one of Diana's favourite motifs and they've become a Kate signature, too. There are dozens of pictures showing the two women in similar outfits. But the most compelling polka dot comparison came in March 2020, when the Duchess of Cambridge wore vintage for the first time on a tour to Ireland. The Oscar de la Renta number was very 1980s, with its pie-crust collar and fuchsia hue.

It was also very reminiscent of a pink spotted Donald Campbell dress that Diana debuted during a visit to Perth, Australia in 1983. The style had returned to the public consciousness a few months before Kate wore her version, after images from filming of the fourth season of Netflix's *The Crown* showed actress Emma Corrin (cast as Diana) wearing a recreation of the look.

**OPPOSITE LEFT** The Duchess of Cambridge in an Alexander McQueen navy velvet evening gown at Buckingham Palace in December 2019.

**OPPOSITE RIGHT** Princess Diana in navy velvet Victor Edelstein at a dinner at the White House in November 1985.

**BELOW LEFT** Kate in vintage Oscar de la Renta at the Museum of Literature, Dublin during the Cambridges' visit to Ireland in 2020.

**BELOW RIGHT** Princess Diana in a pink polka dot dress by Donald Campbell on a visit to Perth on a royal tour of Australia in 1983.

**OPPOSITE** The Duchess
in Erdem for a visit to
the Victoria and Albert
Museum in October 2018.

# a new
# FASHION CHAPTER

On 10 October 2018, the Duchess of Cambridge arrived at the Victoria
and Albert Museum to open its new photographic centre. It was her
first evening engagement after her maternity leave and royal fashion
watchers were eagerly anticipating a fresh dose of Duchess glamour.

As images landed, it was apparent that a sleek, sophisticated New Kate had emerged from her chrysalis. Drilling down, the indicators were all sewn into her new Erdem tweed dress. The neckline was jaunty, the length was neither knee length nor maxi (her previous preferred proportions), the hem was fluted and frayed and the decorative elements were extensive yet strikingly well balanced: a burgundy ribbon just above the natural waistline (a favoured technique of master tailors to whittle the slimmest part of the torso and elongate the legs), a cluster of floral brooches and crystal buttons. And there was more! A new pair of sumptuous Merlot-coloured velvet Jimmy Choos made their debut, as did opulent huge-for-Kate crystal and pearl earrings, also courtesy of Erdem.

It wasn't a complete departure from her established codes – there were still recognizable facets of the Duchess's usual image, from the bouncy blow-dry to the small, boxy clutch – but this was a wow moment with serious subtext: 'I'm back, I'm dialling things up a notch and just because I'm now a mother of three doesn't mean I can't remould the meaning of Princess Glitz.'

That Kate's comeback look coincided with a time when Meghan had been asserting herself as the Royal Family's glittering new star might have had something to do with the Duchess's style rethink. This could have been interpreted as the closest that she has come to a Diana-esque 'revenge dress', but her message was more nuanced than simply dressing to prove a point.

That Erdem dress was not an aberration, but instead the first installment in a carefully revealed series of tweaks. It was a style reinvention that signalled a new phase not only in the Duchess's wardrobe, but in how she behaved and was viewed as one of the most compelling members of the Royal Family.

'She decided at some point that she wasn't going to be overly influenced by fashionistas, that she had her comfort zone and she was going to expand that comfort zone, but she was going to have a uniform; you could predict at any given time what she was going to wear,' reflects Susan Kelley, founder of What Kate Wore, the website that catalogues every detail of every look in which the Duchess of Cambridge has ever been photographed. With this in mind, she instantly noticed Kate's late 2018 upgrade and the surprises it brought. 'What you see now is a woman who respects and understands the different aspects of her role, so she's more comfortable taking risks. Clothing can be like an armour, it can protect oneself from the slings and arrows.'

The Duchess's look had always been put together with an eye on girl-next-door appeal. There was nothing to frighten the horses – or the courtiers – but everything was also in keeping with her own natural fashion instincts. No royal should ever kowtow to the whims of fashion insiders or the temptation to transform into a dedicated fashion plate; that way lies division, alienation and the abandonment of any shred of 'I'm just like you, honest' integrity. But there were huge advantages to this refined new chapter. It created a frisson of excitement, it made Kate appeal to women with whom she hadn't really registered before (there was certainly an influx of fashion-minded types suddenly perplexed at their

**OPPOSITE** Kate in a Gucci blouse and Jigsaw trousers and carrying an Aspinal of London handbag for a visit to the Henry Fawcett Children's Centre in Lambeth, London, March 2019.

**RIGHT** In Alessandra Rich for a visit to Bletchley Park to view a special D-Day exhibition in May 2019.

admiration of the Duchess's looks) and, most vitally, it empowered her anew in her work as she became more engaged than ever with mental health and early years development.

The broad brushstrokes of Kate's new groove included a select few new purchases that breathed new life into her wardrobe; a pair of Katharine Hepburn-like wide-legged trousers marked a joyful departure from the skinny styles that she'd previously preferred. In fact, wearing trousers with any regularity at all in a formal context was a milestone. A lot of impact came from teaming fashion-forward accessories with pieces she already owned; swapping clutch bags for top-handled styles sourced everywhere from small accessible labels like Manu Atelier to heritage brands such as Aspinal, and being more adventurous with shoes, choosing designs that had a little more personality while still blending gracefully with everything else.

There was major excitement on the day in March 2019 when Kate made the walk from her car into a children's centre in London into her own personal runway, showcasing a lilac pussy-bow Gucci blouse teamed with Jigsaw trousers and one of her new Aspinal bags. She looked professional, polished and grown up in this cleverly composed ensemble, which is unlikely to date (the pieces are all timeless classics) but also looked meticulously of the moment.

The Duchess's step change worked to suggest that she had a refreshed verve; classic riding boots gave way to an edgier chunky hiker boot style and she wasn't afraid to toy with what now looked and felt 'appropriate'. Visiting Bletchley Park in May 2019, she donned a 1940s-inspired polka dot tea dress that read as supremely prim with its long, cuffed sleeves and buttoned-up collar. But as Kate sashayed past the crowd which had gathered to greet her, the almost-ankle length dress swooshed open to reveal a mid-thigh split. You could hardly call it rebellious, yet by Duchess standards it certainly felt like it might be.

She has continued to raise the bar and redefine what it means to dress like a royal today. Kate hasn't quite ventured into some of the fashion territories explored by Europe's most stylish royal women – Queen Letizia of Spain has made leather leggings one of her essentials, while Crown Princess Mary of Denmark loves a jumpsuit – but her love of all things ladylike and feminine has been rebooted with extra spark.

Another spectacular display of New Kate came during March 2020's Ireland visit, when the Duchess's tendency to flatter her hosts with her wardrobe choices became a dazzling combination of diplomacy and trend-ticking. Kate brought a selection of new frocks with her in suitably emerald hues, the most memorable of which was a cocktail dress by The Vampire's Wife, a small yet influential label founded by former model Susie Cave, wife of the singer Nick Cave. Accessorized with a pint of Guinness, it was one of the Duchess's cleverest – and coolest – looks to date.

That description has rarely been befitting of a Duchess who has always been keen to look appropriate and conscious of her place at all times. But with growing seniority, poise and confidence, Kate showed that she's now in a position to make her own royal fashion rules.

**OPPOSITE** The Duke and Duchess of Cambridge attend a reception at the Guinness Storehouse's Gravity Bar, Dublin, hosted by the British Ambassador, on their visit to Ireland in 2020. Kate wears The Vampire's Wife.

# Fashion firsts

First tour look: Erdem in Canada, June 2011.

First maternity evening look: Emilia Wickstead at the National Portrait Gallery, April 2013.

First hat as a royal: Cappuccino beret by Philip Treacy, Epsom Derby in June 2011.

First outing for her favourite Smythe navy blazer: June 2011 (and she's worn it 11 times since, most recently in February 2020).

First tour look with Prince George in tow: Catherine Walker & Co in New Zealand, April 2014.

First trousers (that weren't skinny jeans): Gap ikat trousers, September 2016 in Cornwall.

First time Kate wore the Lover's Knot tiara: December 2015, Diplomatic Corps Reception.

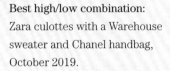

Best high/low combination: Zara culottes with a Warehouse sweater and Chanel handbag, October 2019.

First time she wore Gucci: June 2017, at the V&A.

## *Kate's staples*

**Striped tops** Kate is known to own 10 Breton tops, three of them from Me+Em

**Skinny jeans** Kate owns 12 pairs of skinny jeans

**Black polo necks** Kate has worn black polo necks 15 times for public engagements

**Dresses** Kate owns 236 dresses

**Favourite dress lengths:**
    Knee length: 93
    Midi length: 81
    Above the knee: 56

**Kate's 5 most-worn colours:**
    Blue 236 times
    Black 122 times
    Green 114
    Red 88
    White 83

**Number of times Kate's worn a coat dress: 74**

**Number of coat dresses owned by Kate: 44**

**Kate's oldest coat dress:** Day Birger et Mikkelsen lemon jacquard, first worn for the wedding of Laura Parker Bowles, William's step-sister, in May 2006 and worn 5 more times since.

**Number of Alexander McQueen items Kate owns: 77**

**Number of times she's worn 'nude' shoes: 125**

# INDEX

# PICTURE CREDITS

Page 1 Shutterstock; 2 left Shutterstock; 2 right Tim Rooke/Shutterstock; Page 4 Shutterstock; Page 5 top right Tim Rooke/Shutterstock; 5 bottom left David Hartley/Shutterstock; 6 Shutterstock; 7 Shutterstock; 8 Shutterstock; 9 Shutterstock; 10 Tim Rooke/Shutterstock; 13 Malcolm Clarke/Daily Mail/Shutterstock; 14 bottom left, Shutterstock; 14 top right, Richard Young/Shutterstock; 15 Rupert Hartley/Shutterstock; 16 Eddie Mulholland/Shutterstock; 17 top left Paul McErlane/EPA/Shutterstock; 17 bottom right Sipa/Shutterstock; 18–19, Gero Breloer/AP/Shutterstock; 21 Tim Rooke/Shutterstock; 22 Geoff Pugh/Shutterstock; 23 Shutterstock; 25 Shutterstock; 26 Tim Rooke/Shutterstock; 29 Nils Jorgensen/Shutterstock; 30 Shutterstock; 32 Tim Rooke/Shutterstock; 33 Beretta/Sims/Shutterstock; 34 Shutterstock; 35 Shutterstock; 37 Shutterstock; 38 Shutterstock; 39 Shutterstock; 41 left Shutterstock; 41 top right Shutterstock; 41 right centre Shutterstock; 41 bottom right Shutterstock; 42 top left Shutterstock; 42 bottom left Tim Rooke/Shutterstock; 43 top right Stephen Lock/Shutterstock; 43 bottom right CHRIS JACKSON/POOL/EPA-EFE/Shutterstock; 44 Shutterstock; 46 Tim Rooke/Shutterstock; 48 Charlie Riedel/AP/Shutterstock; 49 Shutterstock; 50 Tim Rooke/Shutterstock; 51 Tim Rooke/Shutterstock; 52 Tim Rooke/Shutterstock; 54 Shutterstock; 55 Tim Rooke/Shutterstock; 57 Tim Rooke/Shutterstock; 58–59 CHRIS JACKSON/POOL/EPA-EFE/Shutterstock; 61 Shutterstock; 63 Tim Rooke/Shutterstock; 64 Shutterstock; 65 Gerry Penny/EPA/Shutterstock; 66 Shutterstock; 67 Shutterstock; 68 Shutterstock; 70 Tim Rooke/Shutterstock; 71 top right, ITV/Shutterstock; 71 bottom left Tim Rooke/Shutterstock; 72 Tim Rooke/Shutterstock; 74 Dominic O'Neill/Shutterstock; 75 INS News Agency Ltd/Shutterstock; 77 Shutterstock; 78 Alan Davidson/Shutterstock; 79 Shutterstock; 80 Tim Rooke/Shutterstock; 81 top Tim Rooke/Shutterstock; 81 centre Stephen Lock/I-Images/Shutterstock; 81 bottom Tim Rooke/Shutterstock; 82 Shutterstock; 83 Tim Rooke/Shutterstock; 84 Tim Rooke/Shutterstock; 85 Tim Rooke/Shutterstock; 86 left Shutterstock; 86 top right Tim Rooke/Shutterstock; 87 Alan Davidson/Shutterstock; 88 Tim Rooke/Shutterstock; 89 Tim Rooke/Shutterstock; 90 Tim Rooke/Shutterstock; 93 Shutterstock; 94 Shutterstock; 95 Shutterstock; 97 Shutterstock; Tim Rooke/Shutterstock; 99 Shutterstock; 101 Shutterstock; 102 Shutterstock; 103 ROBERT PERRY/EPA-EFE/Shutterstock; 104 Shutterstock; 106 Shutterstock; 107 Tim Rooke/Shutterstock; 108 Geoff Pugh/Shutterstock; 109 top left John Shelley/Shutterstock; 109 right Nils Jorgensen/Shutterstock; 110 Shutterstock; 111 Robin Utrecht/Pool/EPA/Shutterstock; 112 Rupert Hartley/Shutterstock; 113 Tim Rooke/Shutterstock; 114 Shutterstock; 115 Shutterstock; 117 Jeff Gilbert/Shutterstock; 118 Rupert Hartley/Shutterstock; 119 Shutterstock; 120 Matt Baron/Shutterstock; 122 Shutterstock; 123 Shutterstock; 124 Shutterstock; 125 Chris Jackson/Shutterstock; 126 left Shutterstock; 126 right James Gourley/Shutterstock; 127 Shutterstock; 129 Charlie Riedel/AP/Shutterstock; 130 Shutterstock; 132 top David Crump/Daily Mail/Shutterstock; 132 bottom Mark Large/Associated Newspapers/Shutterstock; 133 top Shutterstock; 133 bottom Shutterstock; 134 Tim Rooke/Shutterstock; 135 top Tim Rooke/Shutterstock; 135 bottom NEIL HALL/EPA-EFE/Shutterstock; 136 top left Shutterstock; 136 bottom right Tim Rooke/Shutterstock; 139 Shutterstock; 140 Shutterstock; 141 Tim Rooke/Shutterstock; 142 Shutterstock; 143 Shutterstock; 144 Shutterstock; 145 Shutterstock; 146 Shutterstock; 147 Tim Rooke/Shutterstock; 148 Shutterstock; 149 Tim Rooke/Shutterstock; 150 Shutterstock; 151 NEIL MUNNS/EPA-EFE/Shutterstock; 152 Shutterstock; 153 top David Hartley/Rupert Hartley/Shutterstock; 153 bottom CHRIS JACKSON/POOL/EPA-EFE/Shutterstock; 154 Shutterstock; 156 Shutterstock; 158 top Reginald Davis/Shutterstock; 158 bottom Mike Lloyd/Shutterstock; 159 Tim Rooke/Shutterstock; 160 NEIL HALL/EPA-EFE/Shutterstock; 161 Mike Forster/Daily Mail/Shutterstock; 162 left Shutterstock; 162 top right Shutterstock; 163 left Shutterstock; 163 right Shutterstock; 164 James Shaw/Shutterstock; 166 Shutterstock; 167 Tim Rooke/Shutterstock; 168 Shutterstock; 170 top left Tim Rooke/Shutterstock; 170 top centre Tim Rooke/Shutterstock; 170 top right Nils Jorgensen/Shutterstock; 170 bottom left Shutterstock; 170 bottom right Mark Large/Associated Newspapers/Shutterstock; 171 top left Tim Rooke/Shutterstock; 171 top right Shutterstock; 171 bottom left Shutterstock; 171 bottom right Rupert Hartley/Shutterstock; 176 Beretta/Sims/Shutterstock.

# ACKNOWLEDGMENTS

I owe huge thanks to everyone who has shared their stories of dressing and working with the Duchess for this book, especially for doing so in the midst of the Covid-19 lockdown.

The book is brought to life by so many beautiful images – thank you to the photographers who took them.

I am very grateful to my agents Heather and Elly for their endless enthusiasm, and to Annabel, Toni, Cindy, Leslie and Julia for making my idea a reality.

To my bosses and colleagues at *The Telegraph*, who have been so supportive of this project, thank you for being almost as obsessed with royal fashion as I am.

To Hillary, Louise, Vicki and all my brilliant friends and family, thank you for all the advice and support.

Thank you to my Mum, for introducing me to *Hello!* magazine all those years ago, and for your wise words.

And to Johnny – now the world's most unlikely Duchess of Cambridge expert – you're the best.